Edited Book

A BEGINNER'S GUIDE TO VERMICOMPOSTING

Editors

Ms. Kokila Muniyandi
*Department of Microbiology, Faculty of Science, Annamalai University,
Annamalai Nagar, Chidambaram, Tamil Nadu, India*

Dr. Ganesh Punamalai
*Department of Microbiology, Faculty of Science, Annamalai University,
Annamalai Nagar, Chidambaram, Tamil Nadu, India*

Published by

JPS Scientific Publications
India

Published by

JPS Scientific Publications, Tamil Nadu, India.
E.mail: jpsscientificpublications@gmail.com
Website: www.jpsscientificpublications.com

Published in India.

International Standard Book Number (ISBN): 978-81-950475-2-9

ISBN: 978-81-950475-2-9

Contents

1

INTRODUCTION

In recent years, disposal of organic wastes has caused serious environmental hazards and economic problems. Burning of organic wastes contributes tremendously to environmental pollution thus, leading to polluted air, water and land. This process also releases large amount of carbon dioxide in the atmosphere, a main contributor to global warming together with dust particles. About 2,350 years ago Aristotle has said, "Earthworms are intestines of the earth" Only in the twentieth century has the truth in these statements been verified and found correct. He was ahead of our times by two and half of millennia. Darwin was another one to state. "No other creature has contributed to the building of earthworm". Organic waste is defined as any biodegradable waste that originates from animal or plant sources. Organic waste streams include sewage and fecal sludge, agricultural waste, food processing waste, and a fraction of municipal solid waste and it is the largest typology of waste generated globally. It accounts for the largest fraction of municipal solid waste; it has been estimated that globally 598 million tonnes of organic municipal solid waste are generated annually (Hoonweg and Bhada-Tata, 2012). The authors estimate that human population produces 800 million tonnes of organic waste annually, in the form of feces. This waste requires treatment to process and recycle nutrients, and to reduce the negative environmental impact when released into the environment. Additionally, unplanned release of unprocessed organic waste can pose a public health risk due to the spread of pathogens. Although difficult to quantify, it is believed that a majority of the world's organic waste goes untreated, with an estimated 350 million tones of untreated human feces annually discharged into the environment. Therefore, there is an urgent need for the large-scale adoption of sustainable organic waste processing technologies.

Worm-based processing of organic waste is known as vermicomposting, a process developed in the late 1970s. This term did not appear in scientific literature until 1980, but now an extensive body of research exists. Scientific interest in this organic waste processing technology has grown rapidly *e.g.* only seven papers were published in the 1980s, but over 338 have already been published this decade. Vermicomposting has now been used to transform a wide range of organic wastes,

from agricultural residues (Lim *et al.*, 2015) and animal wastes (Lalandera *et al.*, 2015), plant waste (Abassi *et al.*, 2015) food wastes. municipal solid waste (Singh *et al.*, 2011) through to sewage sludge (Sinha *et al.*, 2010; Yadav and Garg, 2011) and industrial wastes (Singh *et al.*, 2011). Vermicomposting is a highly attractive approach for the treatment of organic waste due to low investment cost and the speed of processing, compared with other waste treatment technologies (Abbasi, *et al.*, 2015, Lim *et al.,* 2016). Additionally, the nutrients in the organic waste are recycled into a high value soil amendment known as vermicompost (Lim *et al.*, 2014, 2016, Wu *et al.*, 2014). Recently there has been renewed interest in this technology (Abbasi, *et al.*, 2015, Jiang *et al.*, 2016, Lim *et al.*, 2014, 2016), this due to the inherent sustainability of the technology.

Earthworms are known to sequester carbon through stabilization, hence their action mitigates climate change (Zhang *et al.*, 2013). Vermicomposts are defined as the organic matter of plant and animal origin consisting mainly of finely-divided earthworm castings, produced non-thermophilically with biooxidation and stabilization of the organic material, due to interactions between aerobic microorganism and earthworms, as the materials pass through the earthworm gut. Vermicomposting technology is one of the best options available at present for the treatment of organic wastes. The term vermicomposting is coined from the Latin word *Vermis'* meaning the worms". Vermicomposting refers to natural bioconversion of biodegradable garbage into high quality manure with the help of earthworms. Earthworms play a key role in soil biology; they serve as versatile natural bioreactors to harness energy and destroy soil pathogens by feeding voraciously on all biodegradable refuse. They are nature's way of recycling organic nutrients from dead tissues back to living organisms (Darwin, 1881). Good quality compost production in ambient temperature can be accomplished in a shorter time by the process of vermicomposting that involves the use of proper species of earthworms. The native cellulase activity of earthworms and microorganisms in earthworm gut promote faster decomposition of ingested organic material. The combined effect of enzymatic activity and grinding of organic materials to fineness by earthworms produces the vermicomposting and this is not observed in compost pits without earthworms. Vermicompost, apart from supplying nutrients and growth-enhancing hormones to plants, improves the soil structure leading to an increase in water and nutrient holding capacities of soil. Fruits, flowers and vegetables, and other plant products grown using vermicompost are reported to have better keeping quality. A growing number of individuals and institutions are taking an interest in the production of vermicompost utilizing earthworm activity. Composting of agricultural and animal wastes in the pits before applying to the land is the traditional practices followed

from time immemorial. The materials dumped get tightly packed without proper aeration and with the generation of lots of heat. Further, after allowing material for a sufficient period (3 to 4 months), the composting will not be complete and hard to degrade materials remain unaffected. To solve these problems, scientists have developed a system of waste conversion into valuable materials.

Earthworms are considered as agents to restore soil fertility. The earthworm is physically an aerator, crusher, mixer, chemically a degrader and biologically a stimulator for the decomposition of organic wastes by earthworm consumption is known as vermicomposting. So the vermicompost is anaerobically degraded organic matter which has undergone chemical disintegration by the enzyme activity in the gut of earthworms and also of the enzyme of the associated microbial population. Large quantities of organic residues are available which can be made well-decomposed organic manure through the use of earthworms. Nowadays, vermicompost is becoming well known organic manure due to its nutritional and biological properties. The conventional and most traditional method of composting consists of an accelerated bio-oxidation of the organic matter as it passes through a thermophilic stage (45° to 65°C) where microorganisms liberate heat, carbon dioxide, and water. However, in recent years, researchers have become progressively interested in using another related biological process for stabilizing organic wastes, which does not include a thermophilic stage but involves the use of earthworms for breaking down and stabilizing the organic wastes.

Composting is a biotechnological process by which different microbial communities convert organic wastes into a stabilized form. During the process, thermophilic temperatures arise because of the heat released due to biological activity. These temperatures are responsible for pathogen inactivation. Composting is an aerobic process that requires oxygen, optimal moisture, and enough free air space and C/N ratio within certain limits. The treatment by composting leads to the development of microbial populations, which causes numerous physicochemical changes within the mixture. These changes could influence the metal distribution through the release of heavy metals during organic matter mineralization or the metal solubilization by the decrease of pH, metal biosorption by the microbial biomass, or metal complexation with the newly formed humic substances (HS) or other factors. These works also included investigations into the possibility of utilizing earthworms for the break down of organic wastes such as animal wastes, vegetable wastes and municipal solid wastes (MSW). Earthworms converwet a portion of the organic matter into worm biomass and respiration products, and expel the remaining partially stabilized matter as discrete material (castings). In this process, earthworms and the microorganisms act symbiotically to accelerate the decomposition of organic

Introduction

matter. The agro-industrial wastes are huge source of plant nutrients and their disposal means the ultimate loss of the resourceful material. At present, these wastes are either grossly underutilized or completely unutilized due to *in situ* burning in the fields or land disposal to the surrounding areas. These individually and cumulatively agro-industrial wastes could effectively be tapped for resource recovery through vermicomposting technology for use in sustainable land restoration practices. Marketing is important, so you must develop a plan for selling your product before you make any serious investment in this new venture.

2
VERMICOMPOSTING

Earthworms are often referred to as farmer's friends and nature plowmen. Earthworms are extremely important in soil formation, principally through their activities in consuming organic matter, fragmenting, and mixing it intimately with mineral particles to form aggregates. During their feeding, earthworms promote microbial activity greatly, which in turn accelerates the breakdown of organic matter and stabilization of soil aggregates. The ability of some earthworms to consume a wide range of organic residues such as sewage sludge, animal wastes, crop residues, and industrial refuse has been fully established. In the process of feeding, earthworms fragment the waste substrate, enhance microbial activity and the rates of decomposition of the material, leading to a composting or humification effect by which the unstable organic matter is oxidized and stabilized. The end product commonly termed vermicompost and obtained as the organic wastes pass through the earthworm gut, is quite different from the parent waste material.

Vermicomposting is a simple biotechnological process of composting, in which certain species of earthworms are used to enhance the process of waste conversion and produce a better end product. Vermicomposting differs from composting in several ways (Gandhi *et al.,* 1997). It is a mesophilic process, utilizing microorganisms and earthworms that are active at 10–32°C (not ambient temperature but temperature within the pile of moist organic material). The process is faster than composting because the material passes through the earthworm gut, a significant but not yet fully understood transformation takes place, whereby the resulting earthworm castings (worm manure) are rich in microbial activity and plant growth regulators, and fortified with pest repellence attributes as well, in short, earthworms, through a type of biological alchemy are capable of transforming garbage into 'gold' (Tara crescent, 2003). Vermicompost is finely divided peat-like materials with high porosity, aeration, drainage, and water-holding capacity. They have a vast surface area, providing strong absorbability and retention of nutrients. Vermicompost contains nutrients in forms that are readily taken up by plants such as nitrates, exchangeable phosphorus, and soluble potassium, calcium, and magnesium. Decomposition of various organic substrates (kitchen waste, agro-residues,

institutional and industrial wastes including textile industry sludge and fibers) into valuable vermicompost has been extensively studied using an exotic earthworm species (epigeic- *Eisenia foetida*) (Garg *et al.,2006)*. Tests have also been conducted combining thermo-composting and vermicomposting to improve efficiency and compost quality (Nair *et al.,* 2006; Khaliq *et al.*, 2006), advocate the integrated use of organic and inorganic nutrient sources with effective microorganisms (EM) for improving crop yield. The effects of earthworm processed sheep-manure (vermicompost) on the growth, productivity, and chemical characteristics of soybean straw (*Glycine max* L. Merril.), wheat straw (*Triticum aestivum* L.), maize stover (*Zea mays* L.), chickpea straw (*Cicer arietinum* L.), city garbage and greenhouse tomatoes (*Lycopersicum esculentum*) has also been studied. Earthworm species such as *Eudrilus eugineae* are voracious feeders of organic wastes, and their presence has been found to reduce the time required for composting.

2.1. Raw materials for Vermicomposting

The residues like sugarcane trash, press mud, sugar factory effluent, broiler ash, spent wash, etc, should be bio processed and added to the soil, to complete their natural cycle. By recycling of these residues through vermiculture biotechnology reduces the use of chemical fertilizers derived from non-renewable sources (Venkatachalaiah, 1996). developed the method for collecting, transporting, and composting vegetable and fruit wastes. "BIO AGRO" compost was produced from the city garbage. By the addition of neem cake, rock phosphate, and gypsum in small quantities to this compost "BIO AGRO RICH" compost was made. Organic wastes such as poultry manure, cattle dung, pig manure as well as agricultural waste like sugarcane trash were fed to earthworm to hasten the process of decomposition (Karthikeyan *et al.,* 2007) reported that the waste consists of decomposable organic matter with a high carbon-nitrogen ratio. Hence the organic matter wastes are composed of the vermicomposting process to convert the organic waste into bio-compost. Swati Pattnaik and (Vikram Reddy *et al.,* 2009) reported that the vegetable market waste is leftover and discarded, rotten vegetables/fruits and flowers wastes in the market are daily agro wastes. This urban waste can be converted to a potential plant nutrient-enriched resource compost and vermicompost that can be utilized for sustainable land restoration practices.

2.2 Microbiology of Vermicomposting

Due to the inoculation of microorganisms, the period of composting was reduced by about 4 weeks. The results also indicate that by utilizing mesophilic cellulolytic fungi, the process of composting a high C/N homogenous material can be accelerated and the quality of the resulting in compost can be improved. Various

Vermicomposting

studies also indicated the possibility of augmenting the quality of compost through inoculation with *Azotobacter* and phosphate solubilizing microorganisms in the presence of rock phosphate (Mathur *et al.,* 1986; Edward *et al.,* 1982) studied the symbiotic interaction between earthworms and microorganisms in the breakdown and fragment organic matter progressively. The role of earthworms as vectors of beneficial soil bacteria and their capacity to influence the population dynamics and impact of microorganisms on soil and plants was studied. Actinomycetes and bacteria (both cellulolytic and ligninolytic) which are important in waste degradation increase exponentially along the entire length of the tubular bioreactor. The gut isolates included the Actinomycetes, *Streptomyces lipmanii,* and the oxalate degrading bacterium *Pseudomonas oxalates* and anaerobes have not been enumerated from the worm gut but several nitrogen fixers (*Clostridium butyricum, Clostridium beijerinkii,* and *Clostridium paraputrificum*) have been isolated from *Eisenia foetida* casts microbial growth was limited by the amount of available carbon immobilization of phosphate in earthworm casts are probably caused by mainly abiotic processes, carbon mineralization by soil microflora fertilizer with glucose and phosphorous was limited by nitrogen, except in freshly deposited casts (Karsten, 1995; Mathur *et al.,* 1986) states that it gut of earthworm behaved as an epigenetic/anecic species in sugarcane fields in Australia, where it seems to feed on decayed sugarcane liter and deposits its casts on the soil surface (Karsten, 1995) reported that the digestive enzymes and intestinal microflora of earthworms seem to play an important role in the digestion of soil organic matter, the various enzymes *viz.,* amylase, cellulase, xylanase, endonuclease, acid phosphatase, and their activities in the gut of the two selected earthworms *Eudrilus Eugenie* and *Eisenia fetida* (Yasir *et al.,* 2009) showed that changes in the bacterial community play a major role during vermicomposting. In addition to bacteria, fungi especially cellulolytic fungi also play an important role during vermicomposting. The population of cellulolytic fungi was found to be increased during vermicomposting of different organic wastes. Cellulase produced by these fungi plays a major role in the decomposition of cellulolytic materials of organic wastes.

Prabhat Pramanik and Young Ryun Chung (2011) used two wastes as food for two epigeic earthworms (*Eisenia fetida* and *Eudrilus eugeniae*) to standardize the recycling technique of these two wastes and to study their effect on the fungal especially cellulolytic fungal population, cellulase activity, and their isozyme pattern, chitin content and microbial biomass of waste mixture during vermicomposting. Increasing VN proportion from 25 % to 50 % or even higher, counts of both fungi and cellulolytic fungi in waste mixtures were significantly increased during vermicomposting. Higher chitin content in vinasse-enriched treatments suggested

that fungal biomass and fungi-to-bacterial biomass ratio in these treatments were also increased due to vermicomposting.

2.3. Maintenance of Vermicomposting

Take care to maintain an optimum number of Earthworms in the pit /fields. Their population is adversely affected by

a) Use of chemical fertilizers.
b) Use of certain pesticides against soil-borne pests.
c) Inappropriate cultivation techniques, like the use of rotary cultivators.
d) Acidification of soil.
e) Insufficient organic matter in the soil.
f) Always maintain moisture 60 to 65 %.
g) Make the heap in shady and comparatively higher sites.
h) Worms have been known to crawl out of the bedding and on to the sides and lid if conditions are wrong for them. If the moisture level seems all right, the bedding may be too acidic. This can happen if you add a lot of citrus peels and other acidic foods. Adjust by adding a little garden lime and cutting down on acidic wastes.
i) Worms require protection from excessive sunlight, heat, down pouring rain, etc. They grow well under shades.
j) Protect the earthworms in the pit from their enemies like birds, rats, mice, toads, lizards, centipedes, ants, and cockroaches, etc.

2.4 Vermicomposting types

There can be several names designated to vermicomposting. All are the same but vary only with the extent of waste mass to me vermicomposted and composting containers. Some tag with names of mechanical structure used as composting containers *viz.,* vermin accelerator, etc.

2.4.1 Small scale or Indoor Vermicomposting

It is done under covered areas (with a shade viz., cattle sheds, poultry sheds, back yards, underneath temporary thatched sheds, or in containers). It is preferred in the areas where protection from climatic adversaries like high rains, prolonged spells of high or low temperatures (from less than 10Â°F to more than 45Â°F) is required, and predators like ants, rodents, and large insectivorous birds are abundant.

2.4.2 Large scale or Outdoor Vermicomposting

Larger scale vermicomposting may be of two types:

In-situ culturing of earthworms, it may be

    a) Simple promotion of vermi activity in fallow fields after harvesting of crops

    b) *In-situ* development of earthworms in gardens and orchards.

2.4.3 Simple promotion of Vermic activity in fields

In process of simple promotion of vermic activity in fallow fields ridges are to be raised by 8-10" and whole areas are divided into smaller plots following existing ground level. Partly digested (decomposed) wastes, largely uniformly spread over plots. It is watered to keep moist and covered with other decomposable organic wastes like weeds and leaf litter etc. This helps conserving moisture and promotes vermic activity, i.e. soil humification. Over this leaf litter dwelling species of earthworms are introduced along with a thin layer of somewhat mature cow dung manure. This process is allowed to continue for 3 - 4 or more months, but periodic light irrigation or moistening is continued. In some parts of America, such natural vermicomposting is practiced. In India, this may be possible at the community level, *viz.*, on Panchayati lands (like pastures) and forestry plantations, etc. Bhawalkar Earthworm Research Institute (BERI), Pune, India has developed a cost-effective package to promote vermi activity. The package consists of an application of 5 tons of vermi castings per hectare (the basal dose) and the application of a 100 mm layer of mulch over them. Any organic matter like weeds, agricultural residues, manures, city wastes, food processing wastes can be used as mulch. An application of this basal dose of vermicastings produces earthworms, below the mulch within a month. The young ones mature within two months and soon start reproduction. The population soon reaches a maximum level, depending on the carrying capacity of the soil. Predators also help to control their population. An establishment of an earthworm population of 2.1 lakh/ha is considered ideal for soil fertility. In IIT Mumbai vermiculture parks have been established to convert food waste of their canteens into vermicast. Development of Earthworms in Gardens and Orchards. *In situ* development of earthworms in gardens and orchards where the land is not of the plowed often. The organic matter mulch is maintained at the base of the plant and drip/sprinkler irrigation is practiced by these farmers. Most of these farmers developed earthworms in bins and later, as the population of earthworms, started increasing, they released them into plant basins. In such fields, these earthworms are thriving well and the soil living earthworms are also establishing with the formation of an organic layer at the top. Coconut gardens, fruit orchards, and some mulberry gardens are showing a good response to this kind of practice. In the case of

Vermicomposting

cardamon plantations, with the increase in earthworms population, the visit of rodents also increased and they started destroying the pods of cardamom. The farmers should adopt the practice that is suitable to the region and the cultivation practices. It is important to note that what is good for one crop and one region may not be congenial for the other. Large Scale commercialized vermicomposting in open heaps, this may be done with any method suits to local availability of raw material and other requirements.

2.5 Process

The process of Composting crop residues/Agri wastes using earthworms comprises spreading the agricultural wastes and cow dung in gradually built up shallow layers. The pits are kept shallow to avoid heat build-up that could kill earthworms. To enable earthworms to transform the material relatively faster a temperature of around 300 °C is maintained. The final product generated by this process is called vermicompost which essentially consists of the casts made by earthworms eating the raw organic materials. The process consists of constructing brick-lined beds generally of 0.9 to 1.5 m width and 0.25 to 0.3 m height are constructed inside a shed open from all sides. For commercial production, the beds can be prepared with 15 m length, 1.5 m width, and 0.6 m height spread equally below and above the ground. While the length of the beds can be made as per convenience, the width and height cannot be increased as an increased width affects the ease of operation and an increased height on conversion rate due to heat built up 2.2 Cow dung and farm waste can be placed in layers to make a heap of about 0.6 to 0.9 m height. Earthworms are introduced in between the layers @ 350 worms per m^3 of bed volume that weighs nearly 1 kg. The beds are maintained at about 40 – 50 % moisture content and a temperature of 20 – 30 °C by sprinkling water over the beds. When the commercial-scale production is aimed at, in addition to the cost of production, a considerable amount has to be invested initially on capital items. The capital cost may work out to about Rs. 5000 to 6000 for every tonne of vermicompost production capacity. The high unit capital cost is because large units require considerable expenditure on the preparation of vermi beds, sheds to provide shelter to these beds and machinery. However, these expenditures are incurred only once. Under the operational cost, the transportation of raw materials as also the finished product are the key activities. When the source organic wastes and dung are away from the production facility and the finished product requires transportation to far off places before being marketed, the operational cost would increase. However, in most of the cases, the activity is viable and bankable. The following are the items required to be considered while setting up a unit for the production of vermicompost.

2.6 Quantity of Vermicompost to be Applied (Table- 1)

Types of Crop	*Quantity*
Rice, Wheat, Jowar, Bajra, Maize	2.50 tones /ha
Cotton	3.75 tones/ha
Groundnut, Mustard, and Pulses	2.50 tones/ha
Sugarcane	5.00 tones/ha
Potato, Tomato, Brinjal, Carrot, Cauliflower, Cabbage, and Garlic	1.00 - 2.00 tones/ha
Coconut and Mango	4-5 kg/plant (below 5 years) 8-10 kg/plant (above 5 years)
Lime and Pomegranate	3-4 kg/plant (below 5 years) 6-8 kg/plant (above 5 years)
Pumpkin, Papaya, Orange, Pear, and Peach	6-8 kg /plant
Rose, Jasmine, Marigold, etc.	3.75 tonnes /ha or 2-3 kg/plant
Chilli, Turmeric, Ginger	3.75 tonnes / ha
Grapes, Pineapple, Banana	3.75-5.00 tonnes/ha
Plants in pots	250 gm/pot

2.7. Vermicomposting Requirements

2.7.1. Environmental Requirements

The various species of earthworms have different environmental requirements that are necessary for their propagation and continued health. These requirements will inevitably dictate whether one particular "family" of worms will be suitable for culture in any given circumstance. For instance, though many people may be interested in the possibility of raising *Lumbricus terrestris* (The Nightcrawler, or Dew Worm) in the house as a source of fishing bait, this is simply not very plausible when we consider that this particular worm prefers temperatures in the area of 5 – 10 °C. During the heat of the day, this large number of the earthworm family retreats to the depths of his burrow, venturing out only in the late evening, or early morning, the coolest available times. (Burrows have been found to extend to a depth of over 12 feet). Thus, if we wish to culture this animal in the confines of our homes, we will require the ability to regreate at least a part of the available space. Even then, however, the number of additional considerations will eventually convince most people that night-crawlers should be harvested rather than on the other hand, the two most commonly-used worms for vermicomposting, *Eisenia foetida*, and *Lumbricus*

rubellus are the most popular precisely because of the ease in replicating the environmental conditions they prefer. Perfectly suited to an indoor existence, the culturing of these animals presents next to no problem, requiring only a minimum of effort, and presenting no hardship for those of us who share their place of residence. The fact is, in the absence of the normal hazards these worms usually face in their outdoor habitats, they are found to grow faster, stay healthier, live longer, and reproduce at an increased rate indoors. Thus, indoor culture turns out to be heaven for them, and a great benefit to the "Landlord" who will have a great new way to convert his organic waste materials into a wonderful "food" for his plants, lawn, and garden. These requirements can be broken into three main areas, and we will look at each of these in the following paragraphs.

2.7.2. Air (Aeration)

The microbes that turn your yard, farm, and kitchen waste into compost are aerobes, which means that they need air to live (and to do their work to make compost). Compost piles should allow plenty of air into them. This is usually accomplished by using some kind of "bulky" ingredients such as straw, old weeds (without seeds!), etc. If a pile settles under its weight and excludes air, it can also be "turned" to get more air into the pile. Turning is the process of dismantling a pile and rebuilding it in a fluffed-up state - the fluffiness allows air into the pile. Some people turn their piles several times as the piles rot, to keep the pile as aerobic as possible. Worms are not fond of anaerobic bacteria, and if subjected to conditions of that nature, they will either leave the offending area or if they are unable to take this course of action, they will die. Worms need to breathe, just like most other living creatures. The process of osmosis makes a worm rather different than those of us with lungs, but the result is pretty much the same. Gradually, the available oxygen is used up and replaced with carbon dioxide and other miscellaneous waste gases. Unlike those of us who live aboveground, however, the poor little worm is stuck beneath the soil, or bedding, near the toxic fumes. In addition to this, the decreasing amount of fresh oxygen can increase heat, and the increase in heat will result in a similar rise in the oxygen requirements of the worm. Fortunately, the whole situation is easily rectified and only requires very infrequent attention. About once every two or three weeks, the top few inches of the bedding should be gently stirred, allowing for the escape of any built-up gases. This will also go a long way toward preventing the bedding from becoming too densely packed. The lower levels of the bedding can also be stirred, but on a far less frequent basis. If you are in the habit of burying the food you are placing in the worm-bin, it is quite possible that the bedding is already being stirred sufficiently, and all you need to watch out for in that case is the accidental saturation of the bin. If you are just in the process of setting up a new

Vermicomposting

system, you should keep in mind that a larger surface area is beneficial in this regard. In the case of simple promotion of vermi activity in fallow fields, aeration is not at all a limitation.

2.7.3. Moisture Content

The bin contents should be kept moist but not soaked. Do not allow rainfall to run off a roof into the bin. This could cause the worms to drown. A straw converting may be needed in exposed sites to keep the bin from drying ours during hot summer weather. If we consider that the earthworm (contrary to what its name implies) is a creature of the water, it is not hard to accept that moisture constitutes the most urgent of its requirements for life. However, the problems most often incurred in a worm bed involve too much moisture, rather than not enough. As in most things in life, a suitable balance must be found and maintained for optimum performance, keeping in mind that this balance may have to be altered to accommodate specific needs. Let us first take a look at the lower end of the moisture scale. Under natural conditions, the greatest abundance of earthworms will be located in soils which average between 12 % and 30 % moisture content. If this amount of available moisture should fall too low, the earthworm will begin to occur which, if unchecked, will eventually result in the death of the animal. During the final stages of dehydration, a worm will even expel coelomic fluid from within itself in a desperate attempt to moisten its own body. At this point, total submersion in water may be the only way to prevent the worm's demise. A situation of too much moisture is very often arrived at when a newer breeder, or vermiculture, attempts to keep the worm bedding consistently, and evenly moistened. Observing that the top layer of the material is dryer than it should be, more water is added to the bed. Adequate moisture is essential for microbial activity. A dry compost pile will not decompose efficiently. If rainfall is limited, it will be necessary to water the pile periodically to maintain a steady decomposition rate. Enough water should be added to completely moisten the pile, but overwatering should be avoided. Excess water can lead to anaerobic conditions. Water the pile so that it is damp, but does not remain soggy. The compost will be within the right moisture range if a few drops of water can be squeezed from a handful of material. If no water can be squeezed out, the material is too dry. If water gushes from your hand, it is too wet. When you first placed the worms in their new home, the bedding was made up of fresh material, which in due course would become simply another ingredient in the final product. Then food was added, and the worms went about their usual business of eating everything in sight, altering the material as it passed through their remarkable little bodies, and finally excreting it back into the bed from which it will eventually be harvested, and used to feed the plant. A worm is unable to remain healthy if forced to live in his waste

material. Thus, we change the bedding regularly, preventing the castings from reaching a level where they would be toxic to the bin's inhabitants. By overwatering, however, we speed up the process, spreading the castings with the run-off. (The substance, which will eventually kill the worms, is also the same substance that we wish to save for the plants, and a lot of this can be lost in the excess water).

2.7.4. Temperature

The temperature requirement for optimal results is 20 – 30 °C. However, the survival of earthworms is even at lower temperatures and up to 48 °C air temperature. Obviously, with little provision of shade, the temperature within the worm feed substrate (material to be vermicomposted) can be reduced. For this, the substrate should be tightly packed in containers. Active decomposition happens at average outdoor summer temperatures. While higher pile temperatures will speed the rate of decomposition, it is not true that compost piles have to be hot to decompose properly. The worms survive a fair amount of variation in their climate. The same problem can occur in reverse. If you have the worms out on the balcony for instance, and fearing an early frost you move them from a temperature of 5 °C into the heated living room, try not to be surprised if you later notice that a lot of the survivors are in mourning for missing loved ones. The most suitable temperature range for *Eisenia foetida* and *Lumbricus rubellus* have been shown to fall between 13 – 22 °C, a range, which is also quite convenient for those of us who live with them. Temperatures which fall outside this range can affect the worms in several different ways, not all of which are as final as death. As the temperature drops below 10 °C, the amount of food eaten by the worms will also decrease. The worms will be less active and possibly move a little lower into the bedding (unless it is a cold floor causing the problem, in which case they will move nearer the surface. at 4 or 5 °C, the adult worms may stop producing cocoons, and the growth rate of the younger worms will diminish. Redworms can survive a wide range of temperatures (40 – 80 °F), but they reproduce and process food waste at an optimum bedding temperature range of 55 - 77 °F. The worms should never be allowed to freeze. Bins kept outside may have to be insulated with straw in the winter to keep the worms from freezing. Portable bins can be kept by a water heater in the garage during the winter to keep them warm. It is important to note that if the worm-bin has sufficient moisture content, the temperature in the bedding will average anywhere from 5 to 10 degrees lower than the surrounding air. There are times when this will be an important consideration.

2.8 Advantage of Vermicomposting

a) Vermicompost boosts the growth of plants making them strong and healthy and free from pest attacks. It helps microorganisms produce polysaccharides, improving soil health.

b) Vermicompost absorbs 10 times more water than the soil, so it increases water retention capacity, thus avoiding erosion. Earthworm plows through 7-8 times a day, making the soil loamy, thereby enhancing drainage. They also take in 10 times their body weight in water and release it to the soil when needed.

c) Vermicompost organic elements decompose so finely into 0.2-micron size in the earthworm's stomach enabling roots of plants to easily absorb these food elements.

d) Vermicompost contains abundant food elements; micro bacteria and humus, making it complete manure. Using Vermicompost thus not only saves money but also increases yield by 40 % to 80 % per hectare.

e) Vermicompost increases the shape, color, taste, and luster of crops. It increases shelf life and nutrition of fruits, vegetables, cereals, and flowers.

f) Vermicompost is about 50 % cheaper than chemical fertilizers, saving expensive imports. This will give support to the export of chemical and pollution-free produce to foreign countries thereby earning valuable foreign exchange to the country.

g) Vermicompost increases immunity to crops. Therefore, no money is spent on unaffordable chemical fertilizers, pesticides, and insecticides. Consuming fruits, vegetables, and grains, grown thus is safe and everyone is free from health hazards.

h) Vermicompost is suitable for all types of soil, crops and can be used in any season.

i) Vermicompost is rich in several micro floras like *Azospirillium, Actinomycetes, and Phosphobacillus,* which multiply faster through the digestive system of earthworms.

j) Several enzymes, auxins, and complex growth regulators like *Gibberellins,* which are not formed in different soils and environmental conditions, are present in the earthworm castings.

k) Buffering action neutralizes soil pH.

l) Vermicompost helps multiplication of earthworms, which reduces the incidence of nematodes.

m) Due to buffering action, minerals and trace elements become available more easily to crops.

n) Leaching of nutrients from chemical fertilizers in the soil is reduced considerably especially of Nitrogenous fertilizers.

o) Reduce soil toxicity by buffering action.

p) Vermicompost influences the physiochemical and biological properties of soil where in turn improves soil fertility.

q) Low cost to produce in comparison to fertilizers.

r) Easy to use in comparison to fertilizers.

s) Harmless to useful soil organisms.

t) Converts organic matter to use plant food.

u) The fresh Vermicompost will have maximum microbial load beneficial to increase soil microflora.

2.9 General problems in production of Vermicomposting

The best approach is prevention by always burying the food waste you will discourage fruit flies. Keep a tight lid on the container you use to store waste before adding them to the bin. This will prevent flies from laying eggs in the scraps. This does not help if your kitchen is infested with fruit flies, in which case all the peels of your kitchen fruit will have fruit fly eggs. It is unlikely that your worm bin will have an unpleasant odor. If it does, there several possible causes and steps you can take to remedy the problem.

a) You have overloaded your bin with too much food waste.
   Solution: Don't add any more food for a week or two.

b) The bedding is too wet and compacted.
   Solution: (i) gently stir the entire contents to allow more air in and stop adding food waste for a week or so. Make sure that your food waste is still buried; (ii) The lid can be removed or left slightly ajar to allow the contents to dry out.

c) Your bin is too acidic.
   Solution: Add some calcium carbonate and cut down on the amount of citrus peel and other acidic food waste.

2.9.1. Vermicomposting Material

Earthworms can be fed all forms of food waste, yard, and garden waste, paper, and cardboard, etc. Yard wastes, such as leaves, grass clipping, straw, and non-woody plant trimmings can be composted. Leaves are the dominant organic waste in most backyard compost piles. If grass clippings are used, it is advisable to mix them with other yard wastes, otherwise, the clippings may compact and restrict airflow. Branches and twigs greater than ¼ inch in diameter should be put through a

Vermicomposting

Page
16

shredder/chipper. Kitchen wastes such as vegetable scraps, coffee grounds, and eggshells may also be added. Sawdust may be added in moderate amounts if additional nitrogen is applied. Approximately 1 kg of actual nitrogen is required for 100 kg of dry sawdust. Wood ashes act as a lime source and if used should only be added in small amounts (5 kg per ton of waste). Ordinary black and white newspaper can be composted; however, the nitrogen content is low and will consequently slow down the rate of decomposition. If a paper is composted, it should not be more than 10 % of the total weight of the material in the compost pile. The biologically degradable and decomposable organic wastes commonly used as composting materials in vermiculture and vermicomposting are as follows

2.9.2. Animal dung

Cattle dung, sheep dung, horse dung, goat dung, and poultry dropping, etc may be used for this purpose. In the use of animal dung other than cattle dung, various preliminary testing and precautions for pathogens and responses to earthworms are necessary. The uses of horse dung should be done carefully because the tetanus germ is common in horse dung and is lethal to human beings.

2.9.3. Agricultural waste

Agricultural waste obtained after harvesting and threshing may be used. They include stem, leaves, husk (except paddy husk), peels, vegetable waste, orchard leaf litter, processed food wastes, sugarcane trash and baggase; and processing wastes. Forestry wastes These are plant products such as wood shavings, peels, sawdust, and pulp. All these besides various types of forest litter can be used. The unutilized forest waste such as leaf litter may also be used for Vermicomposting. City leaf litter, the burnt leaf litter from avenue or residential areas may be used, however, reports are not available. If it is used, this would keep cities clean and would provide a useful product. The leaf litter of mango, guava, grasses, and certain weeds (free from seeds) may be used, but we need more information on this aspect. Waste paper and cotton cloth etc. these are decomposable organic waste. If they are not being recycled for other useful products can be recycled with vermicomposting.

2.9.3.1. City refuse

City refuse or garbage on daily production basis comprise important items of city factors and a considerable portion of city refuse can be sorted and recycled or composted. Most of the households as kitchen waste with little manipulation can be used for vermicompost.

2.9.3.2. Biogas slurry

After the recovery of biogas, if not required for agricultural use in conventional composting or can be used for vermicomposting.

2.9.4. Industrial wastes

The industrial wastes like waste from food processing, distillery, etc. can also be used in vermiculture with some manipulations. More specifically following combinations can be used as feed for earthworms for vermiculture and vermicomposting. However, exact proportions may have to be adjusted with little pre-testing.

a) Biogas slurry with some leaf letter and some soil sprinkled over.
b) Cow dung + Sheep droppings + horse dung mixed in equal quantities.
c) Cow dung or mixed dung + Agricultural wastes in the ratio of 10: 3
d) Cow dung or mixed dung + Gram bran in the ratio of 10: 3
e) Cow dung or mixed dung + Kitchen wastes in the ratio of 10: 3
f) Cow dung or mixed dung + Rice polish in the ratio of 10: 3
g) Cow dung or mixed dung + Semi crushed leaf litter in the ratio of 10: 3
h) Cow dung or mixed dung + Sewage sludge in the ratio of 10: 3
i) Cow dung or mixed dung + Vegetable waste in the ratio of 10: 3
j) Cow dung or mixed dung + Wheat bran in the ratio of 10: 3
k) Old cow dung of minimum 7 days
l) Only agricultural waste or sewage sludge or kitchen waste or leaf litter or their mixtures.
m) Weed, leaves, grass clippings + cow dung or table waste + soil 70: 15: 15.

Standard diet by Prof. R.D. Kale includes cow dung or mixed dung + gram bran + wheat bran + vegetable waste in ratios of 10:1:1:1 + some powdered eggshell. Any of the above material combinations can be taken up. These are thoroughly mixed with up turning with a spade to mix. Heaps are watered and kept in shade for partial digestion for 2 to 3 weeks. Then it is beaten to break lumps, i.e. to make it some-what powdery and used as feed for earthworms (preliminary treatment of composting material). In addition to the above, numerous other combinations have been tried and or can be tried with care. For example, de-oiled neem kernel cake can also be used after it has been partially matured or decompose Fresh de-oiled Neem cake has been reported to reduce reproduction and so does sheep dung. Vermi-stabilization is also delayed in some combinations. For all such problems, best is to subject it to initial pretesting. Some weeds and spent or used substrates after

Vermicomposting

mushroom harvest can also be used. Treatment of this material too is the same and is to be mixed with any of the feed materials. The weeds should be free from seeds.

3

CLASSIFICATION OF EARTHWORMS

Depending on their ability to make burrows, earthworms in ecological terms are classified mainly into three following groups.

3.1 Epigeic Earthworms

Earthworms of this group cannot make burrows in the soil. They can only move through crevices of the surface. They are found in aggregates in litter heaps or loose soil with a high level of nitrogen. They feed exclusively on decomposing organic wastes. They remain active throughout the year if conditions are favorable in the environment. *Eisenia fetida* are being used as prominent composting earthworms, two more species namely *Perionyx excavatus* and *Perionyx sansibaricus* are also used for the purpose.

3.2 Endogeic Earthworms

They are subsoil dwellers. They make horizontal burrows than vertical ones. These burrows are not permanent and thus are disturbed during rains. Secretions of the body wall of earthworms cement and smoothen the walls of the burrows and protect the wall from collapsing easily. They move below 30cm or more in the soil.

3.3 Anecic Earthworms

They are found in the soil, which is not frequently disturbed. They make very complicated burrows in the soil and they firmly pack their burrow walls with their castings. With this feed material gets softened in the burrow by the microbial activity, they feed on it. The anecic earthworms like epigeic earthworms are commonly found in temperate countries. In the tropics, they are found distributed in forest and plantation. These are very large. They have a very slow growth rate and long life cycles. They come out from the burrows and drag the ground cover litter into their burrows. They move within 30cm depth from the surface.

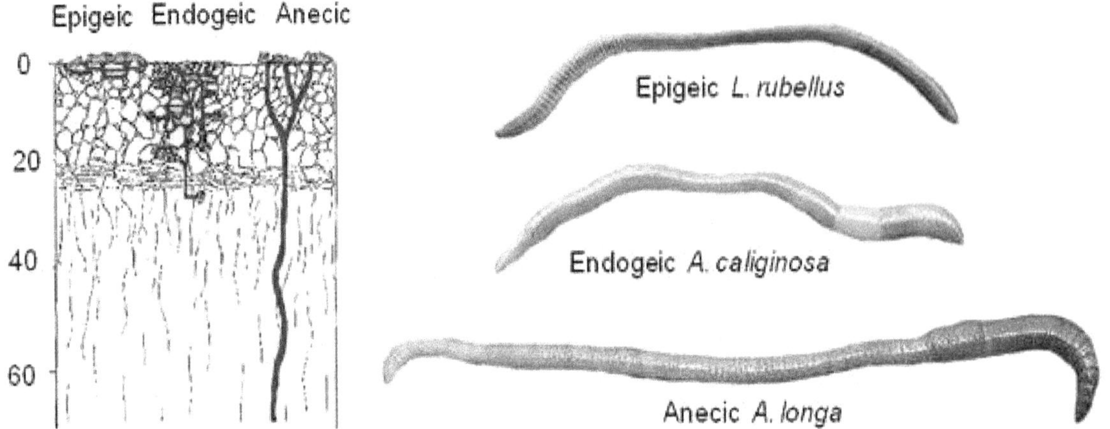

Figure – 3.1: Classification of Earthworms

4

EARTHWORMS USED IN VERMICOMPOST PREPARATION

4.1. *Eisenia fetida*

Eisenia fetida, known under various common names such as redworm, brandling worm, panfish worm, trout worm, tiger worm, red wiggler worm, red Californian earthworm, etc., is a species of earthworm adapted to consume decaying organic material. These worms thrive in rotting vegetation, compost, and manure. They have groups of bristles on each segment that move in and out to grip nearby surfaces as the worms stretch and contract their muscles to push themselves forward or backward.

Figure – 4.1: *Eisenia fetida*

4.2 *Eudrilus eugeniae*

Eudrilus eugenie has originated from West Africa and is popularly called as "African night crawler". They are also found in Srilanka and the Western Ghats of India, particularly, in Travancore and Pune. *Eudrilus eugenie* lives on the surface layer

of moist soil and are also found wherever organic matter is accumulated. It is nocturnal and lies in the surface layer during the day. The worm is reddish-brown with a convex dorsal surface and pale white flattened ventral side. The clitellum is paler than the rest of the body. The adult worms are about 25-30 cm in length, 5-7 mm in diameter, consist of about 250-300 segments and weigh 5600 mg of maximum individual biomass

Figure - 4.2: *Eudrilus eugenie*

4.3 *Lampito mauritii*

This species is referred to in old documents as mega scales Mauritius(King.). It is reportedly common in many parts of South and Southeast Asia.

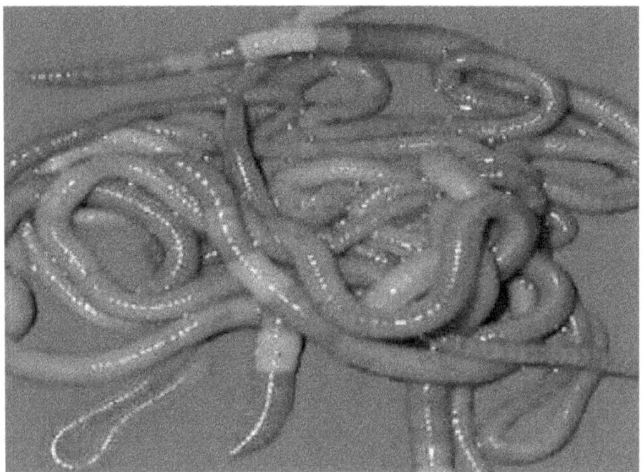

Figure – 4.3: *Lampito Mauritii*

4.4 *Perionyx excavatus*

Perionyx excavatus is reportedly believed to have spread from eastern or western Himalayas downwards in regions of heavy rainfall. It is a commercially produced earthworm. Popular names for this species include composting worms, blues, or Indian blues. This species is marketed for its ability to create fine worm castings quickly. It has recently become more popular in North America for composting purposes. This species belongs to the *Perionyx* genus. This species is suited for vermicomposting in tropical and subtropical regions

Figure – 4.5: *Perionyx excavatus*

5
COLLECTION OF EARTHWORMS

About 500 gm jaggery and an equal quantity of fresh cow dung should be mixed in 15 to 20 liters of water, and this diluted slurry-should be sprinkled over the area. Wet parts of cow dung are scattered over the area and a layer of moistened rice straw should be laid over it. The whole area is then covered with a jute sack. Regular watering should continue for a period of 20 to 25 days and care should be taken to avoid water stagnation. When the cover is removed large worms can be seen. Farmers can collect these earthworms and utilize them for Vermicomposting. A solution of forming @ 0.55 % has been also found effective for the collection of Earthworms. Taking worms out of their natural environment and placing them in containers creates a human responsibility. They are living creatures with their own unique needs, so it is important to create and maintain a healthy habitat for them to do their work.

6

GENERAL ACTIVITIES OF EARTHWORMS

Earthworms occur in diverse habitats. Organic materials like manure, compost, litter, humus, effluents, and kitchen drainage are highly attractive for some species. They are also found in very hydrophilic environs close to both the fresh and brackish waters. Some species can survive under snow and a few are arboreal inhabiting accumulated detritus in the axils of banana, palm, and bamboo trees. Earthworms are omnivorous but they mostly derive nutrition from dead organic matter, which generally does not occur abundantly in the soil. As a result, they are adapted to swallow large quantities of soil for extracting sufficient nourishment from it. The soil-inhabiting protozoans, nematodes, rotifers, bacteria, fungi, etc. have been recorded from the contents of their gut. Earthworms are capable of withstanding considerable starvation with a water loss of up to 70% of their body weight. *Agastrodrilus* (Omodeo and Vailaud,1967) a carnivorous genus of earthworms from the Ivory Coast of Africa has been reported to feed upon other earthworms of the family Eudrilidae (Lavelle, 1983).

The quantity of food taken by a worm varies from 100 to 300 mg/g body weight/day according to Edwards and Lofty (1977). The main activity of earthworms, however, involves the ingestion, in of soil, mixing of different soil components, and production of surface or subsurface castings. The earthworms consume the soil organic matter and convert it into humus within a short period and thereby increase the soil fertility. Within 24 hours they can pass soil almost equivalent to their weight through the alimentary canal. They have therefore rightly been called nature's ploughman. Thus, the soil is being constantly and continuously turned over and over again by these worms and the amount brought to the surface is quite considerable. Annual worn cast production has been. estimated to be between 1.4 and 77.8 tonnes/ha at some Indian sites (Roy, 1957; Dash and Patra, 1979) as compared to 18 - 40 tonnes/ha in English pastures (Darwin, 1881). Larger quantities of 2100-2600 tons/ha have been reported in Africa (Edwards and Lofty, 1977).

Different species produce structurally distinct and taxonomically significant casts: heterogeneous masses, spheroidal to oval-shaped individual pellets small towers of coiled tubes, short threads, and beaded-strings (Julka, 1988). A species of *Tonoscolex* in Burma produces casts that may reach up to 20-25 cm in height. reproduction and cocoon production are possible throughout the year, although maximum cocoon production by Indian species of worms in pasture soils has been recorded in late October and early November (Das and Senapati, 1982). The incubation period varies from species to species. It may be 14 - 30 days for some Indian species as compared to 8.5 to 30 weeks in some European species. Usually, one or two young one hatch from a cocoon, but they may be as many as six in number in *Eisenia fetida* and *Bimastos parvus*. Earthworms possess limited means of active dispersal. Mountains, deserts, and oceans are effective physical barriers for their migration. Some species can move actively for considerable distances during or after heavy rainfalls. In some areas of Western Himalaya, a few litter dwelling species emerge on a mass scale towards the end of monsoons and migrate for short distances in search of suitable environs to tide over unfavorable winter conditions (Julka, 1988). Passive dispersal through stream drift and in mud on the feet of animals and birds has been recorded. Over the years man has also played a significant role, though unintentially, in transporting some species in the soil around the roots of plants. All the lumbricid and a few other species may have been brought to India in this manner. The activity of most earthworms is interrupted during dry periods or under high temperatures. To overcome the adverse period they usually move into the deeper soil layers and may undergo 'diapause' or transform into a quiescent stage. During this period the worm stops feeding and construct a spherical chamber lined with mucus within which it usually rolls into a tight ball or a loose knot. Environmental requirements with an adequate supply of food and availability of moisture the earthworms can thrive very well in all kinds of soils. The type and amount of food influence their population size, diversity, growth rate and fecundity. The tolerance of soil pH varies from species to species. Usually, they can live in soils with pH ranging from 4.5 to 8.7, but neutral soils have greater densities of earthworms as compared to alkaline or acidic soils. The soil temperature and moisture are the other two important factors that influence their seasonality and distribution. In a sub tropical climate like that of India, they are active and abundant mainly during summer rains. Prolonged drought decreases their numbers significantly. A period of about two years is generally required for populations to recover upon the return of favorable conditions. Fluctuations in temperature influence their overall activity, metabolism, respiration, growth as well as reproduction. The ultraviolet rays are injurious and extreme temperatures may often be fatal for the earthworms.

6.1. Effects of Pesticides

Large quantities of insecticides, herbicides, and fungicides are usually applied to soils for controlling different kinds of pests. Some of these chemicals are general biocides that may also kill earthworms besides the target organisms. By and large, they are not very susceptible to pesticides at normal dosages, but at higher concentrations, these toxic substances are absorbed into earthworm's tissues as the soil passes through their intestine while feeding. Residues of heavy metals like cadmium, lead, zinc, and nickel have also been recorded in their bodies The accumulation of toxic chemicals in earthworm tissues is very significant ecologically because these animals are important components in the food chain of several species of birds and mammals.

6.2. Economic importance

To a common man, earthworms are rather insignificant animals which generally come out on the soil surface during the rains and serve as bait for angling. The role of earthworms in enhancing soil fertility was, however, known to even ancient farmers. But with the advent of modern. agricultural practices, during the last 2 to 3 decades, and the use of artificial fertilizers their significance faded. In recent years the farmers are once again realizing the worth of these highly beneficial animals and are making all possible efforts to culture and subsequently release them in fields and gardens.

The beneficial effects of earthworms in increasing soil fertility were documented since the time of Darwin (1881). Soil with higher densities of worms remains loose and has a greater capacity to retain air and moisture. The earthworms by making tunnels while burrowing aerate the earth which helps in increasing the air-holding capacity of the soil. In the act of depositing their castings on the surface at night, they bring the sub-soil to the top and expose it to bacterial action. The bacteria help in the decomposition of cellulose which otherwise does not breakdown easily. The earthworms also take the rich humus from the soil surface to plant roots and thereby help in maintaining soil pH.

Worm castings contain more water-stable aggregates which keep the soils well drained. Soil nitrogen is generally bound in organic complexes and as such is not readily available to plants. This bound nitrogen is converted into available forms like ammonia, nitrates, and nitrites as it passes through the digestive tracts of earthworms. Compared to parent soil the worm casts contain more available nitrate nitrogen, calcium, magnesium, phosphorus, and potassium. Organic matter ingested by the worms is pulverized in their alimentary canal and excreted as a·colloidal

humus which is rich in plant nutrients. Also, a large number of worms die during unfavorable periods when the chemical demand in the soil is maximum due to growing plants. The microbial decomposition of dead worms releases a considerable amount of locked up nitrogen and thereby making it available to the plants. Increase in the organic wastes mainly due to the growth of the human population, agriculture and industry is a global problem and a serious constrain in the maintenance of a clean and healthy environment. Because of their food and feeding habits, the earthworms should be considered nature's most useful converters of these waste products.

Experiments with worms have successfully been conducted for recycling the utilizable organic wastes arising out of household garbage, city refuse, sewage sludge, and paper, food, and wood industries (Mitchell and Homer,1980). Earthworm tissues comprise high amounts of proteins which after proper processing could benefit the livestock and aquaculture by augmenting or replacing traditional feeds. There are also report of worms being eaten by Maoris of New Zealand and the natives of New Guinea (Edwards and Lofty, 1977). In the Indian Unani system of medicine, the external application of preparations made from the dried worms is used in treating wounds, piles, chronic boils, sore throat, hernia, etc., and when taken internally for curing respiratory ailments, jaundice, rheumatic pains, etc. On the other hand, certain habits of earthworms are considered harmful. Some species seize leaves of growing plants and pull them into their burrows, often killing the plants. Their extensive burrowing activity sometimes retards germination, growth, and root development of paddy and some vegetable crops. There are some reports which suggest that earthworms contribute to soil erosion because they bring fine soil particles to the surface. The earthworms are also known to help in the spread and development of some parasites and diseases of both animals and plants. The foot and mouth viral disease of domestic animals is transmitted by earthworms (Edwards and Lofty, 1977). They also act as intermediate hosts of certain parasitic protozoans, cestodes, and nematodes. Several species of nematodes of interesting and phylogenetically primitive types are found as parasites of earthworms.

6.3. Collection, Preservation and Study of Earthworms

Earthworms are found in all types of soils provided there is sufficient moisture and food. They occur in forests, grasslands, arable lands, gardens, orchards, plant nurseries, and greenhouses. They have been living in caves and axils of tree leaves. Organic materials like compost, manure, forest litter and humus, municipal dumps, soils wetted with effluents, and kitchen drainage are highly attractive to some species. Some earthworms are very hydrophilous and a few species can live under

snow on high mountains. They are soft-bodied and require special methods of collection, narcotization, fixation, and preservation for their morphological, taxonomic, and ecological studies

6.3.1. Collection and Preservation

The best method for collecting earthworms is by digging soil with a shovel or spade or any other suitable implement. For a comprehensive survey of earthworms of an area, they should be collected from different ecological niches, *viz.*, litter, kitchen drainage, manure heaps, different types of soils, margins of freshwater bodies, pastures, grasslands, forests, cultivated fields, etc. For morphological studies, it is essential to narcotize live worms before fixation. Several narcotizing solutions are effective, and 5 – 10 % ethyl alcohol or 1 % propylene phenoxetol are amongst the most convenient. Live worms brought from the field are placed in a suitable flat bottomed container with little freshwater. The anaesthetic solution is gradually added to the container until the worms become motionless. When the worms no longer respond to probing they should be transferred to a flat dish containing the fixative solution for at least 24 hours. The most suitable fixative for normal morphological and taxonomic studies is 5 – 10 % formalin depending upon the size of the worm. A 10 % solution of Dowicil l00 (the proprietary name for 1-(3 chorally) 5,7-triaza azoniaadamantane chloride) is also an excellent fixative for earthworms. Specimens fixed in dowicile solution retain their shape and remain quite flexible, showing none of the brittleness often associated with formalin preserved material. Both formalin and dowicile solution is slightly acidic and can be neutralized with limestone or marble chips without affecting the preservative action. Nephridia are best studied by dissecting a freshly narcotized worm in normal saline (0.75 %) solution of Sodium chloride) and fixed *in situ* by covering the whole worm with Bouin's fluid or with acetic bichromate.

Histological studies of earthworms require special attention. The main difficulty encountered in sectioning is the presence of soil in their gut to flush out the soil, worms are fed on wet blotting paper for several days until their feces contain no trace of soil or blotting paper fed worms on sphagnum moss for about 7 days to ensure the voiding of solid particles from the gut (Vail, 1972). The use of sphagnum moss for the maintenance of worms in good condition for a longer period than did wet blotting paper/filter paper, wet paper towels, wet leaves, or just water in a dish. Worms with voided guts should be narcotised and fixed in Bouin's fluid (75 cc saturated aqueous solution of picric acid, 25 cc formalin, and 5 cc glacial acetic acid) or AFA: alcohol-formalin-acetic acid (10 cc formalin, 10 cc glacial acetic acid, 30 cc of 95 % ethyl alcohol, 50 cc distilled water) for microtome sections of an entire worm

or its various organs. Worms are killed by dropping them in 70 % ethyl alcohol for taxonomic studies. When the movement stops, they are removed from alcohol and placed on a piece of blotting paper or any other absorbent paper in a straight position. They are then transferred to a flat-bottomed container with 10 – 15 % formalin for fixation for at least 24 hours. It is essential that worms are straight because curled and twisted specimens are difficult to handle during dissection. The specimens are stored in suitable sized vials or bottles filled with 70 % ethyl alcohol or 5 – 10 % formalin. A label with locality and altitude data, name of the collector, and date of collection is to be added to each vial. For best results, the preservative should be changed within a week, especially for large worms. Sometimes for lack of adequate time in the field, it is not possible to follow this program, it is then recommended to preserve the specimens directly in 4 – 10 % formalin depending on the size of the worm. Fixation of specimens in alcohol is not desirable as they become soft and macerated, and are unsuitable for dissection. Some workers anaesthetize and relax the worms before fixation by placing them in a container filled with water and gradually adding alcohol to it. The main disadvantage of this method is that length of the relaxed specimens maybe twice, thrice or even more than the contracted specimens as obtained by dropping them directly into alcohol or formalin. For the taxonomic description of a species, the latter condition is preferable because uniform contraction is often more easily obtained than uniform relaxation of a worm. Various methods of estimating earthworm populations and habitat preferences are being used. Their effectiveness varies with the species and habitat. No one method is equally suitable for all species and habitats.

6.3.2. Digging, Hand sorting and Wet sieving

Though laborious and time-consuming, this method has been widely used for sampling earthworms with the best results (Edwards and lofty 1977; Reynolds, 1977). Sometimes specimens are liable to be damaged during digging. With the help of a suitable digging tool, cores or quadrates of the soil of exact dimensions are taken for accurate population estimates. Usually, 16 sample units of 25 cm^2 with 20 cm depth provide an adequate estimation of medium-sized worms. For bigger species and deep burrowers, large areas of deeper samples are required. The dug out cores or quadrats are gently broken and the worms are hand sorted and preserved in 5-10% formalin. For better results, the broken soil is washed with a jet of water through a series of sieves for collecting smaller worms and cocoons. The sieved samples are stirred with magnesium sulfate (specific gravity 1.2) solution and a stream of air is blown simultaneously into the solution. After some time, the liberated worms and organic debris float on the surface. In this way earthworm cocoons can be easily collected. Thus, all stages of the population can be sampled by this method.

General activities of Earthworms

6.3.3. Chemical extraction

Various types of chemical extractants have been used for studying earthworm population dynamics. The standardized technique employed for quantitative extraction is based on 0.25 m^2 of soil surface. A solution of 0.55 % formalin (25 ml of formalin in 4.5 litres water) is sprinkled over each quadrat taking care to avoid its run off. The earthworms that surface in 10 minutes following the application of the excellent are collected and preserved in 5 – 10 % formalin for studies in the laboratory. For wet biomass studies, the worms should be washed in freshwater and soak dried over a blotting paper before weighing. Other chemical chloride in 18.25 liters water), potassium permaganate solution (1.5 g liter at the rate of 6.8 liters per m^2), and Mowrah meal have also been used. The advantage with a chemical extraction method is that the sampling time and labor are reduced, a well defined sampling area may be chosen, and there is a minimum disturbance of habitat. But the disadvantages are that only active surface-dwelling species are collected because aestivating or hibernating individuals or some species do not respond to these extractants.

6.3.4. Electrical extraction

A current of electricity passed through the soil also acts as an excellent (Walton, 1933; Deoksen, 1950) used an electric current of 220-240 volt at 3-5A through a 75 cm long electrode for expelling worms from the soil. The only advantage with this method is minimal disturbance to the habitat. The disadvantages are in determine the exact volume of soil treated and the variability of physico chemical properties of the soil. For example, the current penetrates deep into moist soil which brings deep-dwelling species to the surface. There is some danger of too much current killing the worms near the electrodes. The response of different species to electricity may also vary.

6.3.5 Heat extraction

This method operates on the principle of Baermann funnel and may be useful in obtaining small surface-dwelling species that are difficult to the handset (Reynolds, 1977) employed Tullgren funnel and incandescent lights for extracting worms from soil samples brought from the field. This method is again time consuming and has limited use in earthworm sampling.

6.3.6. Vibration method

The mechanical extraction by vibration methods is currently limited to the south-eastern United States. Mechanical stimulation by vibrations seems to have very little effect on Lumbricidae but is extremely successful for some Acanthodrilidae and Megascolecidae species. This often takes the form of a vibrating flexible rod with a bow. The advantages of the mechanical extraction are minimal habitat destruction and the reduced sampling time required for each sample. The disadvantages are the difficulty of defining the exact volume of soil treated, the effects of the variability of the physical and chemical properties of soil, and the variable response of the different species. Several workers have compared the relative efficiency of extracting earthworms by two or more of these methods. Hand sorting or washing gives the best result for most species but is very time-consuming. The formalin method seems to be the best compromise for species with burrows. Formalin extraction followed by hand-sorting to find animals that had not been extracted seems to be the most suitable method for ecological studies (Bouche, 1969).

6.3.7. Method of study

Earthworms cannot be identified without resorting to dissection since their generic or even suprageneric identification is dependent on internal characteristics. Before dissecting a worm, its various external characters like the shape of prostomium, location of genital and nephridial apertures, and from the extent of clitellum should be recorded. It is then pinned in a dissecting dish, containing water, by fine entomological pins at the anterior and posterior ends, taking care to avoid injury to the prostomium. Using a fine scissor or scalpel or even a sharp shaving blade, the body is cut open longitudinally slightly to the left or right side of the mid dorsal line in order to avoid damage to dorsal pores. By carefully cutting septa, the flaps of the body wall are slowly pinned out with fine forceps, preferably first at the post prostatic region and then continuing forward, care being taken to record the exact location of missing and delicate. septa in the gizzard region. To determine the presence of calciferous lamellae and openings of calciferous glands, it is necessary to slit open the esophagous along the middorsal line. The beginning of the intestine and form of typhlosole can be determined by giving a slit just below the mid-dorsal line on one side of the intestine. Penial and copulatory setae are easily removed along with their enlarged follicles from inside, they cannot be pulled from outside without some damage to them. After cleaning the adhering tissue, the setae are mounted on a slide in glycerine or any other media provided the refractive index is sufficiently different from. that of the setae. Canada balsam is not satisfactory for this reason unless the setae are stained. For the study of epidermal setae, a small portion of the

body-wall is cut off with a pair of scissors and treated with a 40% solution of hot Potassium hydroxide (KOH) for 15 - 30 minutes. The skin is washed in water and mounted directly in glycerine after proper dehydration and clearing. To study the digestive system, the gizzard should be cut into two by a longitudinal incision for observing the thickness of its wall and its cuticular lining. In the same way, a portion of the intestine and rectum is also opened from the ventral side to study the morphology and limits of the typhlosole, which lies along the mid dorsal line of the intestine. The excretory system should be examined after fixation of the nephridia *in situ* with Bouin's fluid a septum with attached nephridia is dissected out with needles under a binocular dissecting microscope to separate individual nephridia. The care being taken to keep funnel intact on each nephridium. These are stained and mounted in balsam. Pharyngeal nephridia are studied by tracing their ducts in the pharynx region. Integumentary nephridia are picked up with the forceps and are studied by mounting on a glass slide in glycerine. In a similar manner holonephridia and megameronephridia are taken out from the parietes with the help of forceps for study ·under a microscope. Care should be taken to keep funnel intact. Septal excretory canals and the supra-intestinal excretory ducts are best studied in well fixed and preserved specimens. Preparations of complete septa show the septal excretory canals, while the supra intestinal excretory ducts can be dissected out with needles from the roof of the intestine. The opening of these ducts into the intestine is seen only in sections (Bahl, 1950). For the purpose of sectioning, worms with voided gut and fixed in Bouin's or AFA are used. The dehydrated specimens are cleared with a toluene-terpineol mixture (3:1) and then used alone and embedded in hard paraffin (melting point 60-62° C). The use of xylol and softer paraffin give unsatisfactory results, and many of the sectioning problems (*Eg.* excessive static elasticity, failure of ribbon foundation, shredding of individual sections) are eliminated with the use of toluene, terpineol, and hard paraffin. Embedded tissue is sectioned at 10 μm and the sections are stained with Harri's hematoxylin and alcoholic eosin. In order to obtain coccon, it is best to slect a piece of ground showing casting in April- June or in September- October. Put a heap of earth in a sieve and stir the earth while keeping the sieve in a bucket of water. The earth passes through the sieve while cocoons remain in the sieve along with some pebbles and stones. Cocoons are easily picked up with a camel-hair brush. Cocoons are opened in normal saline by using needles under a dissecting microscope. Embryos of all ages can be obtained and studied by making whole mounts or by sectioning.

6.4. Rearing and Culturing Earthworms

Earthworms feed upon a variety of organic material and could be raised commercially for recycling biodegradable organic wastes, production of biofertilizers, and animal protein for poultry and fish feed. Vermiculture is feasible in suitable containers or specially designed boxes since they are omnivorous, able to withstand environmental changes, and resistant to many diseases. The technology involved is very simple and can easily be adopted in India, especially in rural areas. It is possible to culture worms both indoors and outdoors depending upon the local climatic conditions. The culture boxes or containers should be non-porous to minimize the loss of moisture from the culture medium. The boxes should be made up of lightweight materials like plastic, wood, tin, etc., which could easily be carried from one place to another. The size of the containers may vary according to the need considers a specially designed wooden box to be more convenient and useful. It measures 50 cm in length, 35 cm in width, and 15 - 20 cm in depth. The bottom of the box is provided with a few holes of 50 mm in diameter. The plastic window screen is placed on the inside bottom with burlop or jute cloth lining on top of the screened sides before the culture medium is added. This prevents the culture medium from sticking to the box and escape of worms through the holes but allows the excess of water to drain. The top of the box is covered with a burlop or jute cloth frame. Earthworms can be cultured in commonly available glazed earthen pots, plastic tubs, or even discarded wooden cases, etc., each being covered with a lid made up of plastic or iron window screen. Plastic tubs are considered to be advantageous because these are more durable, lighter in weight, and could easily be arranged one above the other in vertical rows on concrete shelves in limited space. Various combinations of soil and organic matter have been tried for raising worms. A mixture of 1/3 soil and 2/3 organic matter is considered to be more useful in culture containers by Reynolds (1977). Beds in plastic or discarded wooden cases are prepared by spreading a sand layer of 2 - 4 cm in height over which another layer of equal thickness of the soil is added. Organic matter is placed on one side of the container. Water is added to the culture medium to hold 25 - 30 percent of moisture. Indoor cultures are preferably kept in a cool building at a temperature between 10 °C and 15 °C for the lumbricids (e.g. *Eisenia fetida)* and about 20 °C for tropical species (e.g. *Eudrilus eugeniae* and *Perionyx excavatus).* Sources of common organic materials are decayed leaves, hay, straw, rice or wheat bran, vegetable wastes, cow dung, poultry droppings, biogas sludge, etc. Kale (1986) carried out trials of various mixtures of organic matters to study the dietary influence on the biomass and size of the population in *Eudrilus eugeniae.* Young worms fed upon a feed combination of dung and gram bran gained maximum population and dry weight biomass after 3 months of their introduction into the culture medium.

6.5. General Morphology and Characters of Taxonomic Importance

Earthworms are defined as terrestrial annelids with external and internal metameric segmentation throughout the body, without any appendages and suckers but possessing few setae on all segments except the first and last ones. They are hermaphrodite with few gonads in definite segmental locations. They possess a true coelom and closed vascular system. In sexually mature worms, a precisely located epidermal thickening, the clitellum, secretes a cocoon in which ova and spermatozoa are deposited and which are fertilized and develop without a free larval stage.

6.5.1. External Structure

Earthworms are elongate and vermiform in shape. They are usually circular in cross-section but the same forms may be squarish or trapezoidal. An arboreal species of *Perionyx* has a flattened ventral surface. The length and thickness of worm are of limited taxonomic importance since these characters vary considerably within a species. Amputation, regeneration, and methods of preservation also affect their body dimensions. A few species of *Bimastos* (Family Lumbricidae) and *Disaster* (Family Octochaetidae) are less than 20 mm in length, whereas some deep burrowing representatives of *Drawida* (Family Moniligastridae) exceed 1000 mm. Different colors of worms like rich brown, light to dark red, grey, purple, etc. are due to the deposition of pigments in the circular muscles of their body walls. The color should be recorded when a worm is alive since strong fixing fluids generally destroy the pigment. Litter dwellers are deeply, pigmented as compared to inhabitants of topsoil and deep burrowers. The entire body is divided externally into a series of distinct segments by furrows. External segmentation of the body corresponds to an internal segmentation. In some fonts, segments may be superficially subdivided into two or three or more annuli by secondary and tertiary grooves. The number of segments varies intraspecifically and this character can be of taxonomic value only when its limits of variations-have been determined in a large number of individuals of each species. For a taxonomic description of a species, segments are numbered by convention in roman numerals i.e. i. ii. iii… (capitalized by some authors) beginning with the peristomium. Intersegmental furrows are designated by the number of segments on either side of a furrow as 1/2, 2/3, 3/4, etc. The first segment with a crescentic opening, the mouth, is the peristomium. It is provided with a small fleshy lobe the prostomium which is located above the mouth. The different shapes of the prostomium are sometimes of taxonomic importance. In mature worms, a conspicuous cylindrical band of glandular tissue known as the clitellum is present at some distance from the anterior end. Its shape may be either annular (extending all round the body) or saddle-shaped (restricted to dorsal and lateral sides of the body).

General activities of Earthworms

The location of clitellum varies between families/genera/species. *Dravida* spp. (Family Moniligastridae) have the clitellum extending over segments xxiv and include male genital pores. In Megascolecidae, Acanthodrilidae, and Octocbaetidae the clitellum begins at or in, front of xiv, and posteriorly it may include male pores Lumbricidae have the clitellum behind male pores beginning on segments xxvii, xxviii, and extending over four to ten segments. Characteristics of all earthworms are the short hook-like retractile chaetae or setae embedded in the skin with which they hold gain on the substratum during burrowing and locomotion. The positions of setae provide significant reference points for describing the location of taxonomic characteristics like genital and nephridial pores, grooves, genital marketings, etc. Often setae in the region of genital tumescences, male thecal pores are modified in size and shape. Those associated with genital tumescences are known as genital setae, those with male/prostatic pores as penial setae and those with spermathecal pores as copulatory setae. The arrangements of setae according to their number are expressed as lumbricine (8 setae per segment in 4 pairs, e.g. *Drawida. Octochaetona, Eutyphoeus,* etc.) or perichaetine (more than 8 setae per segment, e.g. *Amynthas, Metaphire, Perionyx, Lampito,* etc.). Rarely, the setal arrangement may be lumbricine in anterior and middle regions, and perichaetine in the posterior region of the body as in a few species of *Wahoscolex* from Coorg area of Karnataka (Julka, 1988). In taxonomic descriptions, individual setae are designated by italicized letters, *i.e.* in the lumbricine arrangement by *a, b, c, d*... beginning with the most ventral one and in the perichaetine arrangement by a, b, c, d, e,… beginning with the most ventral setae and z,y,x,.. beginning with the most dorsal one irrespective of the actual number in the ring (Julka, 1988).

A series of tiny openings, the dorsal pores, are located along the mid-dorsal line in the intersegmental furrows. These pores lead directly into the body cavity. The location of first dorsal pore varies in intraspecifically. Dorsal pores are usually absent in worms with aquatic or subaquatic habitats *(Drawida* spp. and most of the ocnerodrilids). Different types of genital pores are located on the ventral surface of earthworms. The position and size of these have long been employed as taxonomic characters. In the Ocnerodrilidae, Acanthodrilidae, Octochaetidae and Megascolecidae, the male pores are associated with the prostatic pores (openings of the ducts of prostates, accessory reproductive glands). The prostatic and male ducts may open to the exterior either separately or as combined pores. The basic conditions of these openings are acanthodriline (male pores on xviii, prostatic pores on xvii and xix, all pores in seminal grooves), microscolecine (prostatic pores alongside or combined with male pores on xvii), Ballantine (prostatic pores alongside or combined with male pores on xix) and megascolecive (prostatic pores along side

General activities of Earthworms

or combined with male pores on xviii). Male pores in some forms are located on papillae of various shapes or at tips of intromittent organs. Entire lumbricid worms the male pores are often located on segment xv, and in the Moniligastridae these pores are one or two pairs in intersegmental furrows 10/11, 11/12 or 12/13. The female pores are most commonly- a single pair, either in an intersegmental furrow or on a segment. They are tiny in size and their position is often diagnostic of a particular family. Thus, they are on segment xiv or its homoeotic equivalent in the Lumbricidae, Octochaetidae, Ocnerodrilidae, Acanthodrilidae, and Megascolecidae, and in the Moniligastridae they are either in the groove 11/12 or on segments xiii or xiv. Sometimes the female pores are united into a single median pore. The location and number of spermathecal pores vary between families and species. They may be paired or sometimes combined to form single median series of pores. In some species *(Bimastos parvus),* they may be absent. A few species like *Eisenia fetida* and *Ocnerodrilus occidentalis* may have ethical morphs. *In Polypheretima- elongate,* spermathecae are more than one pair in each segment. The openings of the integumentary meronephridia (nephridiopores) are microscopic apertures and cannot be easily recognized. But nephridiopores in some holonephric species are quite obvious and their axial position provides important distinguishing characters. Certain epidermal areas on the ventral surface of sexually mature worms are some.times modified in the form of markings, tumescences, ridges, pits, tubercula pubertatis, etc. (Bahl, 1950; Edwards and Lofty, 1977; Julka, 1988).

6.5.2. Internal Structure

The body wall consists of an outer thin non-cellular membrane of the cuticle, epidermis, circular and longitudinal muscle layers, and coelomic epithelium, which separates the body wall from the coelom. The coelom or body cavity is filled with a fluid and is divided at each segment by a septum at the intersegmental furrow. Most of the septa are provided with minute apertures which permit the coelomic fluid to pass freely between segments. Some of the septa in the gizzard region in some species may be much thickened or absent. The presence or absence of septa in the anterior region is of taxonomic importance. The digestive system comprises a straight alimentary canal extending from mouth to anus, and associated caeca and glands. The anterior most part of the canal consists of a short but muscular, buccal cavity, followed by a pharynx. The dorsal surface of the pharynx is thick, muscular, and glandular. The worm sucks food by the action of the pharynx. A short narrow tube, the oesophagus. passes posteriorly from the pharynx. In most of the megascolecids, octochaetids, and acanthodrilids, the oesophagus is modified to form a very prominent oval structure, the gizzard, in any of segments from v to vii.

The gizzard is a highly muscularized organ for pulverizing the food material. The number and position of gizzards have been used in distinguishing the genera, but their position should be determined carefully as some of the septa in this region are either absent or very delicate which may break as the worm is opened. The gizzard may be rudimentary in some worm's, e.g. *Perionyx* spp. There are two oesophageal gizzards in some octochaetid genera like *Dichogaster, Eudichogaster,* and *Barogaster.* In the Moniligastridae, usually more than 3-5 gizzards are present in xii and posteriad segments. A thin walled storage chamber, the crop, is located at the posterior end of the esophagus and in front of the gizzard in the family Lumbricidae. Various types of calciferous glands are associated with the esophagus in some earthworms. They are highly, vascular organs provided internally with lamellae. Their shape, number, segmental position as well as stalked or sessile, paired or unpaired and extramural or intramural provide useful distinguishing characters. The rest of the alimentary canal is the intestine in which most of the digestion and absorption of food takes place. The internal surface of the intestine is sometimes increased by a large dorsal fold, the typhlosole, which may be in the form of a simple, bifid, or even trifid lamella. Its presence or absence, and anterior and posterior limits are important taxonomically. Some species have small tubular outgrowths of intestinal caeca; their shape, position, number, and whether single or paired are of systematic value. Several pairs of glands, the supra-intestinal glands, are sometimes located on the dorsal wall of the intestine in successive segments at the posterior end of typhlosole (e.g. *Eutyphoeus).* The blood vascular system comprises three main vessels extending almost the entire length of the body. These are a dorsal vessel, closely associated with the mid-dorsal line of the alimentary canal; a ventral vessel between the alimentary canal and nerveord a sub-neural vessel between the nerve cord and the body wall. A supra-oesophageal vessel is present on the dorsal wall of the gut in anterior segments. Paired extra oesophageal and later parietal vessels may be present in some earthworms. The dorsal and ventral vessels are connected in each segment by palled commissures, which in some of the anterior segments are enlarged as contractile 'hearts'. The segmental location of the last pair of hearts is· of taxonomic importance. These may be in segment xi (e.g. Families Ocnerodrilidae and Lumbricidae) or in xii or xiii (e.g. Families Acanthodrilidae, Octochaetidae, and Megascolecidae). The dorsal vessel may be aborted anteriorly in some species of *Eutyphoeus,* while the subneural is absent in several octochaetid genera. There is no formalized respiratory mechanism in earthworms, exchange of gases takes place through the highly vascular moist epidermis. Respiration occurs in the air but worms can exist for long periods in highly oxygenated water (Reynolds, 1977).

The excretory organs of earthworms are a series of coiled tubes called nephridia. They are of various kinds and have recently gained importance in earthworm taxonomy. Different types of nephridia may be found within a species. They may be one pair or more than one pair in each segment. Either type of nephridia may be open (stomate, furnished with a ciliated nephrostome) or closed (astomate). Nephridia are either eonephric with their ducts opening directly to the exterior or enteronephric with ducts discharging into the alimentary canal. Astomate enteronephric holonephridia is not yet known. Meronephridia are either very small (micromeronephridia) or relatively conspicuously enlarged into megameronephridia. Ectal ends of the ducts of holonephridia are sometimes dilated to form nephridial bladders or vesicles of various shapes. The central nervous system comprises a bilobed cerebral ganglion on the dorsal surface of the pharynx, a pair of subpharyngeal ganglia, a pair of cricopharyngeal connectives and a ventral nerve cord. The cerebral ganglion is connected to the subpharyngeal ganglia by the circum pharyngeal connectives. The ventral nerve cord runs beneath the alimentary canal close to the body wall from the subpharyngeal ganglia to the last body segment. Superficially the ventral nerve cord appears to be single, it is made up of two longitudinal fused cords. Behind the fourth segment, the nerve cord is swollen in each segment to form a ganglion, from which arise three pairs of segmental nerves that extend around the body wall. At present characteristics of the nervous system have not been used in the earthworm taxonomy.

The reproductive organs consisting of testes, ovaries, seminal vesicles, spermathecae, and prostatic glands have long been used as the main source of taxonomic characters. The basic arrangement of the gonads in the megascolecoid worms (Families Ocnerodrilidae, Acanthodrilidae, Octochaetidae, and Megascolecidae) is paired testes in segments x and xi on posterior faces of septa 9/10 and 10/11, paired male funnels on anterior faces of septa 10/11 and 11/12, and· paired ovaries in xii and xiii (hologyny). The number of testes may be reduced to a single pair (meroandry); a condition with one pair of testes in segment x is termed as protandric, and when in segment xi it is called a metric. The number of ovaries may also undergo reduction i.e. one pair of ovaries in segment xii (progyny) or xiii (metagyny). The testes and male funnels may lie free in their segments or enclosed in' special coelomic chambers, the testis sacs. Septa of the testis and ovarian segments may be evaginated to form the seminal vesicles and ovisacs respectively. The shape, size, number, and segmental location of these structures are of systematic importance. The male funnels open into straight or coiled male ducts, the vasa deferentia. In holandric forms, the anterior and posterior male ducts on each side extend backward and may unite with each other before opening to the exterior or

may discharge independently on the body wall. They may open directly on the body wall (as in *Octochaetona)* or through the prostatic glands (as in *Amynthas. Metaphire).* The posterior end of the vas deferens is sometimes enlarged into an ejaculatory bulb (e.g. *Hoplochaetella).* Accessory reproductive organs, the prostates, are associated with the posterior ends of vasa deferentia in most families of earthworms. Prostates are tubular in shape with a central canal as in the Octochaetidae, Ocnerodrilidae, and Acanthodrilidae or are of racemose shape without a central canal as in the Megascolecidae. In the Eudrilidae, these glands are in the form of outgrowths from the male ducts and are called as 'euprostates'. In the Moniligastridae, the prostates (also termed as male atria) have an outer and an inner glandular, and a middle muscular layer, the latter forming a prostatic capsule. Prostatic glands are absent in the Lumbricidae. The spermathecae are sac-like organs opening ventrally in some of the anterior segments and receive 'the sperm of the other worm during copulation. A spermatheca, typically, consists of an ental sac-like ampulla, a duct by which it opens to the exterior and one or more diverticula usually arising from the duct. Spermathecae in some worms may be absent or diverticulae. The structure, arrangement, and position of reproductive organs in other families of earthworms are different as compared to the megascolecoid worms. One or two pairs of testes and male funnels are enclosed in interseptal sacs in the Moniligastridae. Spermathecae are one or two pairs with long tubular ducts in this family. Internally accessory glands may be associated with genital markings, tubercula pubertatis, copulatory and genital setae. The shape and size of these glands are of taxonomic value.

6.6. Earthworm Diversity

The first records of earthworms in the Indian subcontinent were provided by Robert Templeton in 1844 when he discovered a new species of *Megascolex (M. caeruleus)* from Sri Lanka. Subsequently, several species have been discovered from the subcontinent by various workers notably (Rosa, 1894; Michaelsen, 1909; Stephenson, 1914, 1920, 1921; Gates, 1929, 1930, 1931, 1932, 1933, 1945; Julka, 1976a, 1976b, 1978, 1981). The collective studies of Indian oligochaete taxonomists have resulted in the publication of three well-documented taxonomic monographs on these organisms: Fauna of British India and adjacent countries on Oligochaeta by (Stephenson, 1923; Burmese earthworms by Gates, 1972) and Fauna of India or megadrile Oligochaeta (earthworms), Family Octochaetidae by Julka (1988). These monographs are of great utility for the identification of the majority of earthworm species of our region. At present, earthworm fauna (megadrile) in the Indian subcontinent comprises 509 species placed in 67 genera and 10 families. The majority of them are endemic and belong to 47 genera. *Amynthas* and *Metaphire* have endemicity in Burma and Andaman and the Nicobar Islands, but they along with

General activities of Earthworms

other pheretimoids like *Pilhemera* and *Polypherelima* are peregrine in the Indian and Sri Lankan regions. Fauna of the Andaman and Nicobar Islands is more closely related to that of Bunna and Malayasia than to the Indian mainland. About 68 % of known species of earthworms in the subcontinent belong to ten endemic genera with the break up as *Dravida* (79), *Perionyx* (53), Eutyphoeu (43), *Megascolex* (33), *Amynthas* (33), *Plutellus* (32), *Metaphor* (26), *Hoplochaetella* (18), *Tonoscolex* (16) and *Octochaetona* (15). The remaining 57 genera are either monospecific or represented by less than 10 species. Excluding a few widely distributed species, 38 of the endemic genera are only found in this region. The rest of the seven genera have distribution in other parts of the world (species of *Plutellus* and *Megascolex* from the Australian region possibly are not congeneric with Indian species). A few peregrine forms have also been introduced presumably in the soil around the roots of exotic plants. The peregrine genera are distributed among 8 families: Lumbricidae (8), Ocnerodrilidae (4), Megascolecidae (2), Acanthodrilidae (2), Eudrilidae (1), Glossoscolecidae (1). Criodrilidae (1) and Octochaetidae (1). Successful colonization of peregrine species is mainly due to their tolerance to a wide range of ecological conditions and some extent parthenogenetic mode of reproduction in most of them. The extent of colonization of lumbricids has become so extensive in the Western Himalayas that they now dominate over the endemic species at several places.

6.8. Selection or Suitable Species in Vermicomposting

Though faunal resources of Indian earthworms are very rich, it is very important to select the most suitable species for vermicomposting. It is well established that different species of earthworms have different lifestyles which were, finally classified into three categories (Bouche, 1977).

a) *Litter or dung dwellers*: Small in body size; tolerant to disturbance; high rate of cocoon production; short life cycle; uniform coloration.

b) *Epiges*: Dwellers of top organo-mineral soil and construct horizontal and branching burrows; tolerant to some disturbance; moderate to high rate of cocoon production; life cycle intermediate; small to large in body size; weakly pigmented.

c) **Aneciques**: Deep burrowers that construct vertical burrows, cast at the surface, and emerge from burrows at night to draw down organic material; intolerant to disturbance; low rate of the cocoon. production; long life cycle, large in body size; slightly pigmented at anterior and posterior ends. The most suitable species in vermicomposting which can be economically cultivated on a large scale should have following characteristics: the ability to inhabit and feed upon a high percentage of organic matter, tolerance to disturbance and

General activities of Earthworms

fluctuations in environmental parameters, high rate of cocoon production and short duration of the life cycle. The ecologically classified species as epigenetic or endogenic possess many of the features associated with this type of selection. In our region, some peregrine as well as endemic species with these ecological characteristics are available for utilization in vermicomposting. These are

- Family Lumbricidae: *Bimastos parvus, Dendrobaena rubida, Eisenia fetida, Eisenia hortensis.*
- Family Eudrilidae: *Eudrilus eugeniae,*
- Family Megascolecidae: *Amynthas diffringens, Lampito mauritiuo, Metaphire anomala, Metaphire birumanica, Perionyx excavatus, Perionyx sansibaricus.*
- Family Octochaetidae: *Diehogaster bolaui, Dichogaster saliens, Ramiella bishambari, Hoplochaetella khandalaensis, Hoploehaetella sucetoria*
- Family Ocnerodrilidae: *Oenerodrilus occidentalis*
- Family Mogiligastridae: *Drawida will, Moniligaster perrieri*

6.8. Reproductive Biology (Cocoon Morphology, Life Cycle Pattern and Life Table Analysis) in Earthworms

6.8.1. Understanding the organisms through reproductive biology

The process of producing young ones is the subject matter of reproduction. The reproductive process occupy the central position in the bio management programs. Organisms could either be a pest (harmful) or a benefactor (useful) to man. Knowledge of reproductive biology could help to curtail pest organisms and to enhance benefactors. Reproduction in earthworms is not only peculiar because of hermaphroditism but also there is a great paucity of information in this regard. More than 95% of zoologists have not seen earthworm cocoon. No standard textbook describes details of reproductive biology in any single species of Indian earthworms although it serves as one of the basic biological specimens for introductory biology. Presently earthworm is not restricted as a basic biology material but is being established as a basic material for Biotechnology (Vermitechnology). Because of the vast number of species available in India and because of their academic and economic value, understanding of the reproductive biology of earthworms has become very important. This may help for

a) Understanding the organism
b) Cocoon is most suitable for inoculation, storage and transport for vermiculture based biotechnology
c) Bioindication and biocide tests

d) Prediction of the population characteristics in captivity or nature regarding the impact of environmental variables.

6.8.2 Reproduction in earthworm

Olive and Clark (1978) have distinguished three basic modes of reproduction in annelids. Monotelic - in which a species breeds only once during the whole life cycle. Polytelic - in which breeding occurs at several times during their life cycle. Both monotonic and polytelic species have discrete reproduction and are big bang strategists. From the physiological point of view, one could distinguish discrete breeders which undergo reproductive crisis or crises during. a year, from those who breed steadily over a period without such a crisis. The third category is semicontinuous/ continuous where the species breed several times during life and release gametes in a number broods over an extended breeding season within one or more years. Earthworms were grouped among semi-continuous/continuous breeders (Lee, 1985; Cole, 1954; Gadgil, and Bossert; 1970) have classified species that reproduce only once in their lifetime and die as semelparous and those that reproduce repeatedly as 'iteroparous'.

Earthworms are hermaphrodite and each worm produces both ova and spermatozoa. Exchange of sperms occurs during the copulation of two mature worms and results in the production of cocoon -Biparental mode of reproduction is more common method of cocoon production. Copulation has been observed in only a few earthworms. Each species has a number spermathecae in its anterior segments. A little behind the last pair of spermathecae is the female pore which opens to the ventral side. In *Metaphire posthuma* (previously *Pheretima posthuma)* clitellum remains in 14-16 segments. Genital papillae arise on each segment of 17 and 19 and the male generative apertures remain in the 18th segment. The female pore is connected to the oviduct which brings the ova from the ovaries (situated on the posterior surface of septum 2/13) as well as other secretions to it. Each male pore is connected to a thicker tube which incorporates the tube from the testis (the vas, differences) and the prostate gland (Prostatic duct). The sequence of copulation has been given as observed in *Metaphire* sp. The copulating animals lie with the anterior ventral surface facing each other but each head pointing in opposite directions. The male pores of one come in contact with the spermathecal pores of the other. The sperms and the prostatic fluid are mutually discharged into the posterior most pair of spermathecae, where they are nourished by some fluids (Tembe and Duhash, 1961). Each partner moves backward in a sequential manner so as to discharge into the spermathecae insuccessive until all spermathecae are charged. The partners then separate after about an hour. The clitellum of each copulating pair gets enclosed in a colloidal

secretion from the clitellum. The three layered wall of a cocoon is secreted by a type of clitellar gland cell containing large granules (Grove and Cowley, 1926). It contains protein and a chitinoid material which is probably chitin (Needham, 1969). Because of the presence of chitin, initially formed colorless cocoon darkens with exposure to air. Uniparental parthenogenesis with self-fertilization is also known in some earthworm species where as there is absence or retrogression of some secondary sexual organs like spermathecae, prostates, etc. methods of reproduction in some earthworms found in given India.

6.8.3 Reproductive biology of Indian earthworm

Of the earthworms, the reproductive biology of the Lumbricidae is by far the best known from the reviews of (Stephenson, 1930; Satchell, 1967; Edwards and Lofty, 1972; Lee, 1985). But sufficient information was not available on Indian earthworms except in *P. heretima* (now Metaphire) a representative of the important tropical family Megascolecidae, to allow comparisons to be made with lumbricids. Pioneering works on reproductive biology have been reported by (Evans and Guild, 1948 a & b; Gavrilov, 1948; Michon, 1954; Phillipson and Bolton, 1977). The first observation on the reproductive biology of Megascolecidae worm has been recorded (Bahl, 1927, 1950; Oishai, 1930; Tembe and Dubash, 1961). Ecology of the reproductive biology of Indian worms was also reported (Senapati and Dash, 1979; Senapati *et al.,*1979; Dash and Senapati, 1982). This was followed with a series of publications dealing with cocoon morphology, emergence patterns, growth, life cycle, life table, energy allocation to reproduction. (Senapati, 1980; Senapati and Dash, 1984; Sahu and Senapati, 1986, 1988, 1991; Sahu *et al.,* 1988). Other works relating to the reproductive biology of Indian earthworms were also observed (Kale *et al.,* 1982; Kale and Bano, 1985).

6.8.4. Cocoon collection and characteristics

Cocoons of earthworms are in general ovoid capsules, prolonged into short processes at both poles, when fresh they are whitish and very soft jelly-like and later become harder and color varies from lemon yellow to olive green to pinkish-red. The collection of the cocoon is a tedious affair of wet sieving and hand-sorting from the habitat soil. Selection of the sieve depends on the size of the cocoon and generally, a sieve having pore size 500µ is preferred (Senapati and Dash, 1979, 1984; Dash and Senapati, 1980). Cocoons may be stored at the low or high temperature inside an incubator with and without soil medium (Dash and Senapati, 1980). Preservation of the cocoon is the same as that of the worm and could be kept in 5% formalin. However, for chromosomal study, live cocoons may be fixed in 1:3 acetoalcohol from the field sampling generally, three types of cocoons are collected. Live cocoons

having variable colors and when examined under a microscope or magnifying lens show live embryo at different stages of development. Dead cocoon which is generally black. contain putrefied material. Empty cocoon which is the cocoon case having a hollow space might be occupied by foreign organisms like. nematodes, enchytraeids, etc. or foreign materials like soil, etc. (Senapati *et al.,* 1979; Dash and Senapati, 1980).

Earthworm cocoons might possess different types of ornamentation at the tapering ends. The ornamentation might be short as in *Dravida will, Lampito maurtii* or may belong thread like structure as in *Drawida caleb, Glyphidrilus tuberous,* or may be flattened structure as in *Perionyx excavatus.* The cocoons of *Criodrilus* are spindle-shaped with the ends drawn out to about 1.5 to 7 cm long corresponding to the length of the clitellum in this worm (about 32 segments) (Stephenson, 1939). Cocoon of *Megascolides australis,* the largest known earthworm is 75mm in length and 20mm in diameter and contains a single embryo which when hatched is as long as one fool Cocoon of *Metaphire posthuma* is small and is about 2.0 mm in length and 1.5 mm in width. Comparative characteristic features of earthworms and their cocoon from temperature and tropical habitats of the world is given.

Earthworm cocoon after undergoing incubation produces young worms called juveniles that lack genital papillae and clitellum. The incubation period of cocoon varies in different species and also with environmental parameters. The incubation period ranges from 3 to 30 weeks in temperate worms whereas it is 1 to 8 weeks in case of tropical worms. The incubation period of *O. sureness* (4 weeks at about 25 °C and 15 g % soil moisture) could be extended to more than 12 weeks at 20 °C with a 15 g % moisture level. A low incubation period in tropical worms might be an adaptive strategy to cope with environmental drastic change (Senapati *et al.* 1979). The incubation period could be determined in laboratory conditions by keeping fresh laid cocoons on moist filter paper spread over habitat soil. Young worm/worms hatch from the cocoon at the end of the incubation period. Dichogaster below the worm is reported to have the shortest incubation period of about one-week duration at 20 ± 2 g % soil, moisture, and 25 ± 2 °C of soil temperature (Sahu and Senapati, 1986). The incubation period of about four weeks has been reported for *Octochaetona sureness, Lampito Mauriti, Perionyx excavatus, Ponotoscolex corethrurus, Metaphire posthuma* and *Polypheretima elongate* (Dash and Senapati, 1980; Kale *et al.,* 1982; Senapati and Dash, 1982, 1984; Kale and Bano, 1985; Sahu and. Senapati, 1986, 1988, 1991; Sahu *et al.,* 1988). Usually, a single worm emerges out of each cocoon. But in some cases, two to three worms hatching from a single cocoon has also been reported (Dash and Senapati, 1980).

General activities of Earthworms

6.8.5 Earthworms in Nutrient fixation

Soil improvement is very important to make use of even the less productive land to increase food production for the ever-increasing human population. Mineral aggregates are' more stable in the presence of organic particles. Deficiency in organic carbon reduces the storage capacity of soil for nitrogen, sulfur, and phosphorus and leads to atmospheric acidity and reduction in soil fertility. The world's labile source of carbon has to be incorporated into the soil before it escapes into the atmosphere as methane and carbon dioxide. This requires economically and environmentally managed sound procedures. The worm cast in nature is found to contain the highest organic matter content than in those of other major soil fauna like ants and termites have reported a higher electrical conductivity of casts that denotes an increase in the level of soluble salts in the soil (Joshi and Kelkar, 1952). They have also observed the casts to have greater nitrifying power than soils. The increased stability of casts and a considerable amount of carbon and nitrogen than in the parent soil have been observed (Dutt, 1948; Bhaduria and Ramakrishna, 1989). The water-stable aggregates make the soil more aerobic which is considered to be one of the main factors responsible for nitrogen fixation. Though the worm cast is considered to be a strong aggregate, its stability depends on concentration and type of organic matter, bacterial and fungal polysaccharides (Lee, 1985). These findings suggest that earthworms form one of the agents in organic matter breakdown and for the rapid incorporation of detritus into the soil strata.

7

VERMICOMPOST: A BIO-ORGANIC FERTILIZER

Aristotle called earthworms, "The intestines of earth", and considered them as agents to restore soil fertility. Voracious feeding habits of selected species of earthworms on a rich source of organic matter and their high reproductive potential are now being exploited in temperate countries. The nature of food and its availability and other physical parameters like temperature, light and moisture content, biological parameters like the density pressure, environmental conditioning created by their activity influence their growth and fecundity (Evans and Guild, 1948; Mba, 1978, 1983; Neuhauser *et al.,* 1980, Evans and Guild , 1948; Kale and Bano, 1985) also showed that the earthworms preferring a nitrogen-rich diet grow faster and produce more cocoons than those feeding on mineralized soil. Even litter feeding worms show an order of preference for certain leafy matter (Kale and Krlshnamoorthy, 1981). The knowledge on the biology, food habits and habitat selections of worms are important factors for encouraging the culturing of worms for degradation of animal waste, plant residues, and wastes from the food processing units. Biomass production of worms on one hand helps to enhance the process of waste degradation and on the other hand residue free worms can be used as an alternate source of protein for poultry birds and fish. Some earthworms such as *Eudrilus Eugenie, Eisenia fetida,* and *Perionyx excavatus* are found to be very efficient and adaptable in cultures under semi natural conditions in our country.

Various agricultural wastes like post harvest stubbles, sugar cane trash, coir waste, and paper pulp, and fecal matter of cow, sheep, horse, biogas sludge, poultry droppings have been tried as a food source for these worms. It was found that the breakdown of these materials was enhanced considerably in the presence of worms (Kale *et al.,* 1982, 1988; Bano and Kale, 1986; Kale and Bano, 1988). Disintegrable plant remains to form a good source of manure on exposing them to earthworm activity. The degraded organic matter by worm activity is called 'Vermicompost' which can be used as topsoil or organic manure in fields to prevent organic carbon

Vermicompost: A Bio-organic Fertilizer

deficiency and soil erosion. The worm cast is a better source of organic manure over other anaerobically degraded compost because of the following facts. The worm cast is loosely packed granular aggregates of semi-digested matter that provides energy for the establishment of various microorganisms. Some of the microbes which are found in association with the cast are responsible for deodorizing excrements derived from organic wastes with an obnoxious odor (Watanabe *et al.,* 1982). The cast also forms a suitable base for free living beneficial microbes whose activities are essential for releasing nutrients to higher plants (Atlavinyte *et al.,* 1971; Atlavinyte and Vanagas, 1982). Thus, an establishment of the macro environment takes place in the presence of worms in a given media. Especially in tropical countries, earthworms cannot remain active throughout the year. The prevailing environmental conditions and type of soil bring about leaching of nutrients at a rapid rate. The existing microbial population fails to remain active due to a lack of energy requirements for their activity. Under such circumstances, the regular application of worm casts to fields improves the physicochemical and biological properties of soil (Kale, *et al.,* 1990). The worm activated soil or worm cast provides essential nutrients in the available form to plants. Besides biochemical activities of established microbes and worm exudates have stimulatory effect on plant growth. The presence of earthworms in culture pots have a positive effect on germination, growth, and yield of crops (Atlavinyte *et al.,* 1971) have also shown an influence of worm activity on the density of microbes and in vit B12 level in soil (Springett and Syers, 1979) showed an increase in herbage production on the application of worm cast. The yield influencing substances are released into the soil by earthworms, which is a specific character. Irrespective of the species of worms, growth, and yield of crops show a definite increase in wormed worked soils than in controls. An increase in protein synthesis of *Agaricus bisporus* and *Raphanus sativus* has been reported when grown in the presence of worm cast (Galli *et al.,* 1990; Tomato *et al.,* 1990). An increase in uptake of nutrients in the level of available nutrients in symbiotic microbial association with cereals and some ornamental plants was observed in our studies (Kale *et al.,* 1987, 1990). These findings authenticate the possibility of ameliorating soils by application of worm cast or when worked soil wherever the introduction of worms is not feasible. The culture maintenance and vermicompost production form an independent bio-technological unit for mass production of compost.

7.1. Species Recommended for the Technology

The Technology of many species of earthworms tested for mass cultivation all over the world, including the tropical and temperate regions, *Eisenia fetida, Eudrilus eugeniae,* and *Perionyx excavatus* come in the order of preference for their ability to degrade the wastes. Their high biomass production may attain an increase of 40 to 90

times in a period of 3 to 6 months with adequate space and food (Neuhauser *et al.,* 1980; Kale *et al.,* 1988; Kale and Bano 1988; Viljoen and Reinecke, 1989; Mba, 1978, 1983; Reinecke and Hallett, 1989). Frequent harvesting of worms brings down density pressure and enables the continued growth of the worm population. Increased demand for fish meal in livestock' fans has resulted in a continuous escalation of the cost of fish meal. With proper management of vermiculture, the worm protein can supplement a fish meal, and the demand for animal protein can be subdued (Gurrero, 1983; Kale, 1986; Nandeesha *et al.,* 1988; Edwards and Thompson, 1973; Ireland (1977) reviewed the effect of various pesticides and heavy metals on earthworms. It is found that worms can act as "bioconcentration" of heavy metals and other toxic organic compounds. This quality of worms can be made use of to minimize toxins from sewage sludge before applying the same as fertilizer to fields. This will bring down the risk of entry of these pollutants into the plant system and then into the sequential food chain. When worms are used for this purpose, they should be prevented from entering into the food chain as they are found to concentrate very high levels of these toxins in their tissue. Mass rearing and maintaining, worm cultures and tapping of organic wastes for their maintenance have a good scope for developing it as a cottage industry in our country where there is no dearth for organic wastes, congenial climatic conditions, and required manpower. The tapping of resourceful. technology is of utmost importance for the present day as "soil is the placenta of life"

8

VERMITECHNOLOGY IN INDIA

The availability of nutrients for sustained crop production has become a serious constraint in agriculture with the increased cost and shortage of fertilizers. The utilization of organic wastes through the agency of earthworms is important for developing vermicomposting techniques. Earthworms could be made use of to meet needs for plant nutrients, recycling of biodegradable organic; wastes, and in solving problems of deteriorating soil conditions. Vermitechnology is the method of converting wastes into useful products through the action of earthworms. It comprises three main processes:

a) *Vermiculture* - Rearing of earthworms.

b) *Vermicomposting* - Biodegradation of waste biomass in an earthworm way.

c) *Vermiconservation* - Mass maintenance of sustainability of waste lands through earthworms.

Utilizable products and benefits of Vermitechnology are waste biomass management, animal protein production, organic pollution abatement, wasteland conservation, and land reclamation, production of worm-worked manure, soil fertility, and enhancement in plant production.

8.1. Prospects and Problems of Waste management and Vermicomposting

Environmental improvement is an accepted national goal. Because of the low population and availability of inexpensive energy and enough raw materials, recycling of used material was not considered necessary in the past. Moreover, the amount of waste produced was within the optimal, limit, and taken care of by nature. Under the present conditions of the acute energy crisis and environmental degradation due to a steep rise in population, it is very essential to develop suitable technology for' recovery of energy from non-conventional sources like organic wastes which were once thought to be of no use. The concept of resource recycling is

Vermitechnology in India

particularly relevant to agricultural production. The problem of organic recycling in soil improvement and crop production may be tackled by

a) Improvement in the process of composting by a reduction in the processing mode and enrichment in quality.
b) Utilization of available organic residues and inorganic wastes in the natural plant production cycle.

Waste biomass from domestic, agriculture, urban, and industrial sources are the main cause of organic pollution in developing countries. A major portion of refuse, more than 60 percent, constitutes decomposable materials. Nothing is waste and much of the waste is "vegetable matter in the wrong place." Today's waste may be a raw material in the future and waste of one organism may be an energy source for another. India produces about 3,000 million tonnes of organic wastes annually which could be utilized for recovering important resources like fertilizer, fuel, food, and fodder. This huge amount of waste has also the potentiality to produce 400 million tonnes of plant nutrients besides biogas and alcohol (Dash and Senapati, 1986). There are several ways of organic waste biomass treatment and composting is one of the best, suitable, and acceptable ways for a quality environment. Organic manure utilization is useful in

a) Narrowing the fertilizer gap up to about 25 percent.
b) Improvement in water retention capacity and quality of soil by increasing humus content.
c) Besides NPK the supply of other essential nutrients.
d) Reduction in leaching of nutrients.
e) Abatement of organic pollution.

Appropriate disposal of waste is most essential and beneficial from an ecological and economical point of view. Decomposers like earthworms are also "rate-regulators and bio-catalysts at the organism level. They stimulate composting both in enhancing manual value and decreasing time. Application of vermicompost and earthworms increases the yield of paddy crops ranging up to 95 % in grains and 128 % in straw and root (Senapati *et al.,* 1985). The earthworm is physically an aerator, crusher and mixer, chemically a degrader and biologically a stimulator in the decomposition sub system (Senapati and Dash, 1984). Epigeic (surface-dwelling) worms, depending upon high-quality nutrient yield, are good biodegraders.

Vermitechnology in India

8.2. Vermicomposting broadly speaking involves three main phases

a) Collection of wastes, shredding, mechanical separation of metal, glass, ceramics, etc. and storage of organic wastes.
b) Composting of organic wastes by earthworms, organic wastes may be first utilized for the production of biogas and residual slurry added to vermicomposting beds.
c) Sorting of large undecomposed wastes which can be used for landfilling or reprocessing. Earthworms are harnessed for protein production and vermicompost is used as a biofertilizer.

8.3. Prospects and Problems of Waste Land Management and Vermiconservation

There is no simple and short-term answer to complex and long-term problems of agriculture. Long term strategies and food security cannot only depend upon industrialized agriculture which is energy-wise inefficient and unable to preserve the quality of an ecosystem. Wastelands are increasing through a lack of proper management and amount to about 20 percent of a land surface. If implications of high doses of fertilizers and pesticides, industrial wastes, irrigation, and deforestation are considered, the proportions of wastelands will increase significantly. This needs biological ways of improving the soil system. Endogeic earthworms are potential conservators of these systems through their high efficiency of harvesting energy in nutrient poor soil. On the contrary, epigeic worms do not play any role in soil formation and are of no use in the reclamation of wastelands. It is well known that earthworms enhance soil fertility, and attempts have been made to introduce worms in poor soil or to increase their population by adding organic matter or fertilizer. Earthworms have been used in reclaiming flooded areas that are subsequently drained and put into cultivation (Edwards and Lofty, 1977). These worms have been successfully introduced to newly established areas of artesian irrigation in the U.S.S.R. for improving soil formation.

8.4 Vermitechnology Development at Global and National Levels

The concept of Vermitechnology was started in the middle of the twentieth century. The first vermicomposting plant was set up at Hollands Landing, Ontario, Canada. Since then, vermicomposting has been earnestly undertaken in the United States of America, Italy, Japan, and now being initiated in France, Israel, etc. Along with success stories, there are also instances like the Philippines where vermicomposting industries have collapsed because of a lack of social acceptance and extension education. Japan procures about 3000 million tonnes of worms from the U.S.A. to take care of huge paper and spinning mill wastes. Another 180,000

Vermitechnology in India

tonnes/year is required by thousands of eel fanners in that country. Vermiconservation of wastelands is of recent origin and there is a great scope for its development all over the world. Worm forming does not involve a very skilled technology. Worm, young, old, handicapped, literate, and illiterate can easily take it up. In India, vermitechnology is still in the developing stage (Dash and Senapati, 1988) compared the vermiculture characteristics of seven Indian species (including two peregrine and commonly cultured species, *Eisenia fetida* and *Eudrilus eugeniae*). (Kale and Bano, 1986) employed an African worm, *Eudrilus eugeniae,* for the degradation of organic wastes. The casts thus obtained were used as bio-organic fertilizer. Vermitechnology has a bright future in India. Vast resources of unskilled labor and huge quantities of organic wastes could be tapped for this purpose. But important problems of Vermitechnology are

a) Proper species selection
b) Development of procedures depending on local resources and needs
c) Integrated agriculture program along with Vermitechnology
d) Land use constrain and marketing, etc.

8.5. Selection of Suitable Vermicomposting species under Indian conditions

Waste materials are increasing enormously with the growth of the human population, agriculture, and industrialization the disposal of these materials has become imperative for a healthy and quality environment. In this regard recycling of utilizable wastes is feasible. The preparation of organic manure from wastes can immensely help in a rural based economy. It has been demonstrated that earthworms can process household garbage, city refuse, sewage sludge, and waste from paper, wool, and food industries (Hartenstein *et al.,* 1979; Appelbof, 1980; Senapati and Dash, 1982). Earthworms dominate the soil invertebrate biomass (more than 80 percent) in different ecosystems of the world. Various studies on energy channelization through earthworms in tropical environs and the effect of earthworm gut enzymes on the reduction of carbon/nitrogen ratio in soil show that earthworms can be utilized in the decomposition of waste organic biomass (Dash and Patra, 1977; Senapati and Dash, 1982). These organisms can process 10 to 20% of the net energy input into an ecosystem which is an indication of their importance in the decomposer sub ecosystem (Senapati and Dash 1984). Vermicomposting is earthworms' way of sanitation measures for waste biomass. More than 500 species of earthworms occur in India. Out of these, the vermicomposting potentiality of only 3-4 species is known. It is, therefore, very necessary to tap such potentialities of several other species for the development of indigenous Vermitechnology. It may be possible

to select suitable Vermicomposting species for different Indian regions with distinctive climates.

8.6 Biological Scaling Method of Selection

The functional capability of an organism can be measured by biological scaling procedures. Analysis of interspecific variations in earthworms, determination of their life cycle strategy selection pressure and niche segregation will provide useful information for vermiculture, vermicomposting and vermifeed preparation.

8.6.1. *Allometry*

This relates to the relationship between body size and various biological function. Byzova (1965) reports an allometric relationship between the body size and rate of respiration among 6 species of earthworms. A high correlation between oxygen consumption and the size of the pigmented species of earthworms has been observed. On the contrary, this correlation for the unpigmented species is insignificant. Further, small-sized pigmented worms with higher metabolic levels show a horizontal migration in surface soil as compared to large-sized unpigmented ones. The size relationship of earthworms with pH tolerance, sensitivity to ultraviolet rays, nitrogenous excretion, and resistance to desiccation have also been demonstrated. Allometric scaling of poikilotherms like earthworms could be made use of in predicting their potentiality and application.

8.6.2. *Trophic study*

Decomposers have generally been classified as carnivores, microbivores, and saprovores. They are also subdivided into necrotrophs, biotrophs, and saprotrophs. This classification refers to the dynamic relationship between a decomposer and its food. Necrotrophs include some herbivores, plant-parasitic microbes, predators and microtrophs, and have a strategy of short-term exploitation of living organisms which results in rapid depletion of food resources. Biotrophs (root-feeding nematodes, etc.) have long term exploitation of their living food sources that is dependent on the continuous existence of the host. Saprotrophs utilize dead food and the majority of decomposers fall under this category. Trophic characteristics of different forms of earthworms as categorized by Bouche (1977) can be recognized. Epigeic worms are phytophagous, endogeic worms are geophagous and antiques being phytophagous.

8.6.3. Niche segregation

Niche was first viewed as the ultimate distributional unit. Ecologically, it was defined as the functional role and position of the organism in its community. Recently, (Pianka, 1978) has defined the niche as 'all the various ways in which a given organisamic unit conforms to its particular environment (an organismic unit is an individual, a population or a species).' Studies on niche segregation of phytophagous, geophagous, and phytophagous earthworms are useful in identifying suitable species for vermiculture.

8.6.4. Selection pressure

Ecological studies show two types' of distinct population growth equations. Firstly, the populations with unlimited resources and least or no competition, and restricted to a limited favorable time period having a maximum population followed by zero or minimum population. Secondly, the populations relate to limited resources and severe competition and pave continuous occurrences. The evolution of earthworms and their present-day continuation, recolonization, and establishment are associated with. selection pressure of various environmental parameters. Selection pressure seems to have initially favored the short life cycle of surface feeding worms and must have swung as the climate ameliorated to favor the slow and resource-conserving lifestyle of the soil dwellers.

8.7. Implications of Biological Scaling in Vermitechnology

The small body size of epigeic worms associated with high population density, turn over and reproductive rate, and exploitative bioenergetics with a low duration of incubation and life cycle, and thriving on high energy substrate are most suitable for vermicomposting. These are also some of the characteristics of selected species. An African species, *Eudrilus eugeniae,* and *Eisenia fetida,* are being cultured in several parts of the world. These species have also been transported to India, and *Eudrilus eugeniae* is being cultured in South India for producing biofertilizer. Initial studies show that indigenous compost worms like *Perionyx excavatus, Perionyx sansibaricus,* and *Dichogaster bolawi* could also be taken up for vermicomposting. Some species of *Hoplochaetela, Drawida, Lampito, and Moniligaster* may also be considered for utilization in vermicomposting. These species are surface dwellers and deeply pigmented, and the morphology of their alimentary canal (reduced or absence of typlosole) indicated an epigeic way of their life. Certain litter dwelling species of genus *Perionyx, Amynthas,* and *Megascolex* may also be used in the degradation of organic wastes.

9
ORGANIC MATTER IN SOIL

The organic matter, the plant, and animal materials range from bacteria, fungal hyphae, soft leaf tissues to tough woody substances, single celled protozoa, nematodes, soft-bodied worms, and insect larvae, arthropods with tough exoskeletons to large vertebrate animals and excreta. These complex substances are usually made up of carbohydrates, simple sugars, starch, cellulose, hemicellulose, pectins, gums, mucilage, proteins, fats, oils, waxes, resins, alcohols, aldehydes, ketones, organic acids, lignin, phenols, tannins, hydrocarbons, alkaloids, pigments and many other products.

9.1. What is "Organic?"

Anything alive or once was alive is "organic." All plants and animals, anything made from plants or animals, and any wastes generated by plants and animals are organic. Organic products are an important part of the economy and everyone's life. Some of the common organic materials that are used and disposed of daily include food, paper products like tissues, and yard wastes. organic materials account for much of what is consumed and thrown away every day. Paper products alone make up over 19% of human waste. In total, organics make up 52 % of the waste stream! What are the ways to manage the sheer volume of organic wastes produced.

9.2 9.2. Soil organisms and their role in humification of organic matter

Soil is the portion of loose materials that cover the earth's surface on which the plants can grow. The organic nutrients, essential for the growth of plants and animals, are derived from soil These inorganic constituents occur in the parent rock and doing formation of soil these are recombined into forms useable by a large number of diverse organisms (Burges and Raw, 1967; Kuhnelt, 1976). The solid phase of soil has two main constituents, namely mineral material, derived from some parent' material by weathering and organic material. Both of the components undergo a process of decomposition under the action of various physical, chemical,

and biological agents (Wallwork, 1970). Soil Organisms - the Living Community the faunal community in the soil is essentially formed of the following elements:

9.3. Producers

The proper soil does not have the producer which can build up organic material out of inorganic matters. The soil surface and the top layers contain autotrophic plants such as green algae, blue-green algae, and other microforms.

9.3.1. Primary consumers

9.3.1.1 Herbivores

They are poorly represented in the soil. However, some Protozoa *(Amoeba, the amoebae)*, snails of the genus *Carychium* and some mites are essentially recognized as algae feeders. Some hemipteran insects and nematodes are efficient root suckers. There are· other insects like mole crickets, fly and beetles larvae, wireworms, and myriapods which are considered as root nibblers.

9.3.1.2. Fungus1eeders

The mycelia are eaten by a variety of animals like nematodes, some snails and slugs, some myriapods, collembola; a few beetles and oribatid mites.

9.3.1.3. Bacteria1eeders

Many soil Protozoa and nematodes prefer definite species of bacteria.

9.3.2. Detriti jlores

9.3.2.1 Primary decomposers

The bacteria, fungi, Protozoa, some dipteran larvae, isopoda, mites, nematodes, etc. play a very important role as detritivores.

9.3.3. Secondary decomposers

The droppings of all the digesters of fresh plant litter are further decomposed by the secondary decomposers. This group includes earthworms, enchytraeids, diplopods, collembola, and some diptera larvae.

9.3.4.1. Carnivores

Several soil organisms are carnivores. The most important of these are predaceous protozoa, enchytraeids, nematodes, mesostigmatid mites, tabanid larvae, snails, beetles, pseudoscorpions, spiders, etc.

9.4 Decomposition of Organic Matter

Decomposition may be defined as the mechanical disintegration of dead plant or animal remains leading to the formation of humus, when the gross cell structure is no longer recognizable. It may otherwise be clarified as breaking down of complex organic molecules to carbohydrates, water, and mineral components.

9.4.1. Processes of Decomposition

The decomposition of organic matter depends on the physico chemical conditions of the sub soil as well as on the nature of the organic matter (Dickinson and Pugh, 1974). In wet spongy ground where water prevents access of soft ancient air, the process of decomposition is very slow and incomplete resulting in the formation of peat and undecomposed residues accumulate over parent rock. In other cases where the condition is opposite to that of peat formation, the process is known as decay. It is carried out by various organisms like bacteria and beetles. The third category of decomposition is known as putrefaction and occurs in a condition where water is abundantly present and air has little or no access. The fourth· and the most effective process of decomposition is humification where organic matter decomposes in the presence of adequate water and air. The end product of the transformation is a complex substance called humus.

9.4.2. Phases of Decomposition

The plants and small animals having soft tissues are usually decomposed by soil microflora. The tougher and chemically stable tissues are broken down by the action of both soil fauna and microflora (Seastedt, 1984). The organic matter may be decomposed at the soil surface or incorporated directly into the soil for decomposition.

9.5. Decomposition of Plant Organic matter

The chemical constituents of plant litter are generally categorized into cellulose, hemicellulose, lignin, water soluble sugars, amino acids, and aliphatic acids, ether and alcohol-soluble fats, oils, waxes, resins, pigments, and proteins. The

phylloplane fungi attack easily decomposable sugars in the leaf surface. As a result, the leaf becomes senescent, the fungi containing cutinase, pectinase, and cellulase penetrate the cuticle and disintegrate the cell walls. Microorganisms like bacteria *(Pseudomonas, Arthrobacter, Clostridium, Bacillus, Aerobacter,* etc.) and fungi *(Aspergillus, Mucor, Penicillium, Trichoderma, Cladosporium,* etc.) attack the accumulated leaf litter on the forest floor which darkens and becomes weathered. The water-soluble substances, mainly sugars, organic acids, and polyphenols are leached into the soil. As the amount of water soluble polyphenols becomes less due to weathering, the litter becomes more palatable to other decomposers. The palatability varies greatly among the soil invertebrates. An increase in polyphenolic materials precipitate protein complexes in leaves and make them less digestible to the soil fauna. If the tannin content is minimum, the phytophagous insects and earthworms become more active. The microbial activity is followed by mechanical disintegration of organic matter through the action of dipteran larvae, Isopoda, mites, nematodes, tardigrades, etc. The carbohydrates like starch are broken down chemically to produce carbon dioxide or methane, alcohol, and organic acids. the lignins are transformed into smaller substances by bacteria. The protein is split into amino acids which are either utilized by the organisms as food or are further acted upon by microorganisms giving rise to ammonia and carbon dioxide, alcohols, and organic acids. Other nitrogeneus substances are also converted by microorganisms into ammonia and carbondioxide. The second phase of decomposition starts in the presence of earthworms, enchytraeids, millipedes, Collembola, some Diptera larvae, rotifers, and oribatid mites. The major role performed by these soil invertebrates is in the form of fragmentation of litter.

During the initial stages of liver fragmentation, these organisms provide a more suitable physical substrate form, microbial growth. However, certain chemical changes occur during litter fragmentation. The enzymes are secreted by the symbiotic gut flora in some invertebrates breakdown cellulose. Some animals synthesize humic substances in their digestive tract. The fragmentation of litter further accelerates microbial invasion and tissue breakdown initiated by the microflora which in turn favors further attack by other soil animals. The microbes again disintegrate the remaining organic material and a complex substance, the humus, is fonned and this process is known as humification (Edwards *et al.,* 1970). The activities of the fauna and micro-flora are complementary and intricately interrelated. The number of microbes is high in soils with earthworms. The breakdown of organic matter into simpler forms and its incorporation into soil largely depends on the feeding by soil animals alternating with the growth of microorganisms.

9.6. Contribution of Soil Organisms to the Breakdown of Organic Matter

Soil microorganisms and animals contribute to the breakdown of organic matter in various ways:

a) The microorganisms degrade the organic matter through the action of enzymes secreted by them.

b) Animals disintegrate plant and animal tissues, and provide a suitable substrate for invasion by microorganisms.

c) Animals selectively decompose and chemically change the organic residues.

d) Animals mix the organic matter thoroughly.

e) Animals transform plant residues into humid substances.

f) Animals form complex aggregate of organic matter with the mineral part of soil.

g) Role of Earthworms in Humification or Organic Matter Earthworms play an important role in the breakdown of plant litter and incorporate it into the soil.

9.7. Role of Earthworms in Humification of Organic matter

Earth worm play an important role in the breakdown of plant litter and incorporate it into the soil.

9.7.1. Their contribution may be summarized by the following points

9.7.1.1. Removal of leaf litter

The lumbricid earthworms *(Lumbricus the"entries)* are capable of removing up to 90 % of leaf and other litter material through consumption from the soil surface in temperate regions.

9.7.1.2. Litter burial

The castings of many species of earthworms cover the litter, bringing it closer to litter: decomposers.

9.7.1.3. Fragmentation

The earthworms and enchytraeids fragment the litter material, increasing the surface area on which others may feed.

9.7.1.4. Incorporation

The burrowing activities help in incorporating fragmented and decomposed plant material throughout the soil horizons.

Organic matter in Soil

9.7.1.5. Effect on the **C**: *N ratio*

While passing through the gut of earthworms, the ratio of carbon to nitrogen in the ingested plant material is lowered, so that it can be directly assimilated by plants.

9.7.1.6. Effect on the soil microflora

The feces of earthworms contain more microflora than the surrounding soil.

9.8. Major Factors Influencing Decomposition

9.8.1. Temperature

It greatly affects the growth and activity of soil organisms. It is apparently important as an ecological factor for soil fauna as they can respond to temperature changes. Most of the soil microflora are mesophiles and require a maximum and minimum temperature for growth and activity., The thermophilic organisms also need a particular range of temperatures for growth. Many observations indicate that seasonal changes in temperature are related to decomposition rates.

9.8.2. Moisture

The decomposition process is influenced by the amount of moisture in the organic matter as well as in the air. During the drought, decomposition of mull and more litter is. retarded and the number of saprophagous animals is reduced. Several groups of organisms depend on moisture for maintenance of their activity and movement through the soil.

9.8.3. Soil Atmosphere

The aerobic organisms require oxygen for respiration and oxidative assimilation. carbon dioxide regulates the pH of microhabitats which influences the growth of many organisms.

9.8.4. pH

There are remarkable differences in. the microflow and fauna of acid and alkaline soils. It is also obscene that many potential decomposer organisms are less active or inactive when the pH is below 5.0.

9.8.5. Light

This factor is certainly important for heating the soil but it also directly affects the distribution of soil organisms. The negatively phototactic soil animals are

Organic matter in Soil

generally absent from the surface layer of soil. The growth of some fungi is also affected by light.

9.8.6. *Nitrogen content*

The decomposers use carbon as an energy source while nitrogen is assimilated into cell proteins and other compounds. Thus, in the early stages of decomposition high nitrogen content in the organic matter prompts the process.

9.8.7. *Polyphenol content*

Polyphenol content in plant litter decomposition, the polyphenols play a major role. The polyhydroxy phenols in plants comprise 5-15% of their dry weight.

9.9. Manage Organic Materials at Home

People have a variety of options and must make decisions about what is most appropriate for their unique situation. The decision depends on what materials are available, how much time and effort a person is willing to spend, the space available, costs, aesthetic considerations, and what options are available. To make these decisions, one must be familiar with the entire range of home composting methods and the types of materials and maintenance styles best suited to each of these systems. Step one in selecting a management strategy for organic materials generated at home is to understand the available options. When solid waste management priorities are applied to organic materials, the following hierarchy of options results:

- *Source Reduction* - Reducing the amount of yard debris through landscaping strategies and practices.
- *Reuse* - Composting of materials for reuse on-site.
- *Recycling* - Collection of organic materials for processing and marketing by centralized composting facilities.

9.9.1 Source Reduction

Source reduction principles can be used to reduce the amount of yard debris generated. But what options are there for the wastes that come out of yards and gardens When autumn comes, one cannot decide that the leaves won't fall. However, it can be a choice to reduce organic materials generated at home. The choices are fewer than the multitude of choices made at the supermarket, but the process is the same and the results can be just as impressive.

9.9.1.1. Determine Needs

There are three main questions to ask about how yard debris is generated to determine if one "needs" to be producing so much waste. *How is the yard used?* The use affects the amount of space devoted to high maintenance high waste-producing components, such as lawn and annual flower beds, as opposed to low-maintenance plantings or paved areas.

- Is the level of maintenance provided essentially for plant health and a reasonable appearance of the yard. The amount of yard debris created can be reduced by mowing, watering, and fertilizing less.
- What materials can be put to use at home that is currently being disposed

9.9.1.2. Identify Alternatives

Several steps can be taken to reduce the number of organic wastes generated in home landscapes. The alternative range from simple changes in maintenance procedures to complete re-landscaping of yards to create self-sustaining composting systems.

9.9.1.3. Landscape Waste Reduction Strategies

9.9.1.3.1. Grass cycling

Grass clippings are the largest single component of landscape waste in most yards. Yet it is healthier for the lawn to leave the clippings on the lawn than to remove them. It makes mowing quicker and easier. When grass cycling, it is best to mow every 5 to 7 days in warm seasons. However, in wet weather, it is inefficient to leave the clippings on the lawn. Letting clippings remain on the ground returns nutrients to the lawn, adds organic matter to rejuvenate the soil, conserves moisture, and saves time and money on bagging. Grass cycling does not contribute to the build-up of "thatch," which is an accumulation of dead roots and stems. It helps to have a lawnmower that is designed to "mulch" grass clippings back into the turf. Mulching mowers, now widely available, recirculate the clippings through the blades, chopping them into tiny pieces and blowing them down into the grass. Other mowers may be adapted by modifying the outlet spout to direct clippings down rather than out. Reel-type mowers are also effective at cutting the clippings small enough so that they are not conspicuous when left on the lawn. They are also a great way to reduce pollution! A gasoline lawn mower running for one hour emits the same amount of pollution as 40 new automobiles running for one hour. New reel mowers are light, quiet, relatively maintenance-free, and they don't blow exhaust. More information about reel mowers is available at www.reelmowerguide.com. During periods of fast

Organic matter in Soil

growth and wet weather, grass cycling may require more frequent cuttings to avoid heavy deposits of clippings. When not bagging the clippings, each mowing can take half the time.

9.9.1.3.2. Mulching

Mulching conserves water and protects soil from erosion and compaction. Many common yard clippings make excellent mulches or soft "paving" for paths and play areas. Grass clippings, leaves, and pine needles are all suitable for mulching landscapes. Wood chips from pruning and removing trees are a natural substitute for "Beauty Bark." This material can often be obtained at no cost by calling a tree service. Yard debris mulches can be applied following the same methods described for using compost as mulch. Annual flower and vegetable gardens can be mulched with non-woody materials that break down quickly and tilled under without competing with plants for nitrogen. If woody materials, such as sawdust or wood chips, are used in an annual garden, they must be pulled aside before tilling, or they must be balanced by adding a high nitrogen fertilizer such as blood meal when tilled in. Trees and shrubs can be mulched with one-half to one-inch layers of grass clippings, or with two to four inch layers of wood chips, twigs, or pine needles. If layers of fine green materials are too thick they can mat down, becoming an-aerobic and acting as impenetrable barriers to both air and water.

9.9.1.3.3. Selective Fertilization and Watering

Selective use of fertilizers and water, applied at the correct time in proper amounts, actually makes lawns healthier and more tolerant of stress and produces less waste. Lawns should be fertilized in autumn and winter to encourage strong root development. These strongly rooted plants will grow evenly through the summer with less water. Healthy lawns in the Puget Sound region need only one inch of water per week during dry summer months. Measuring irrigation rates allows watering only as much as necessary.

9.9.1.3.4 Turn in Crop Wastes

At harvest time, crop wastes from annual vegetable and flower gardens can be chopped or tilled into the soil. This returns nutrients and organic material to the soil. Spring crops will decompose quickly if cut when they are still succulent, or nitrogen fertilizer can be added to speed decomposition. Fall crop wastes can be turned in or left roughly cut on the surface to protect soil from erosion and compaction, then tilled in with fertilizers a few weeks before spring planting. Diseased or insect infested plants should not be turned in.

9.9.1.3.5. Lawn Size Reduction

Reducing lawn size produces less debris and conserves fertilizer, water, labor, and other resources. Lawns produce more waste and require more maintenance than any other landscaping. Low maintenance groundcovers or woodland gardens where fallen leaves are naturally recycled produce less waste. These can be used to replace grass in low traffic areas. In many cases, ground covers will be healthier and more attractive than lawns grown in less than optimum conditions, and they require less work to stay attractive. Some common, quick-growing, low-maintenance ground covers include St. Johnswort (*Hypericum perforatum*), Rubus carcinoids "Creeping Raspberry," creeping thyme varieties, beach strawberry (*Fragaria chiloensis*), and barren strawberry (Waldsteinia Willd.). Many low and spreading shrubs also provide interesting alternatives to lawn. Areas used heavily as paths or play areas can be replaced by mulch or wood chips. To create a low-maintenance, long-lasting path or play area, remove the sod and lay down two or three overlapping layers of corrugated cardboard to suppress weed growth. Cover the cardboard with four to six inches of the chip; it will compact as it is walked on. Eco-lawns are another option. Many species of grasses are appealing for lawns but some are more environment friendly than others. Some require less water, fertilizer, and mowing. Other eco-lawns have a mix of plants including grasses, clover, and strawberry so they still provide an appealing, green ground cover but are healthier because of the diversity. Resources are available online.

9.9.1.3.6. Natural Landscapes

Many people replace high-maintenance lawns and shrubs with more natural-looking wooded areas or wildflower meadows. An initial thick layer of wood chips or other yard debris helps to create the woodland look and reduce watering, weeding, and other maintenance. These wood-lands areas also provide a place to use grass clippings, leaves, needles, and other trimmings as mulches. Meadow areas (probably away from the street or borders with neighbours) can be seeded with wildflowers and pasture grasses with attractive seed heads. These meadows are attractive when left unwatered and unmoved or only mowed once each summer after flowering.

9.9.2 Reuse Organics

Sometimes major changes in the layout of a garden or maintenance plan are not possible. In these cases, it is important to carefully select landscaping practices to reduce waste. Some general criteria to use in selecting yard debris management options include:

- Reducing or reusing as many materials as possible at home (or on-site at public facilities). On-site reuse or composting is the most efficient landscape waste management option.

- Using organic materials diverted from other sites whenever possible to meet landscape needs. Consider trading unwanted plants or plant divisions with neighbours and friends. Always try to reuse wastes, such as wood chips and animal manures, before purchasing new materials that would provide the same service.

- Buying compost and mulch products made from recycled yard debris for potting mixes, soil amendments, and other garden needs.

9.9.3. Recycling Organic Materials

Recycling organic materials in most cases means composting. Landscape trimmings and food scraps can be composted at home. There are also commercial alternatives to composting at home.

9.10. Commercial Composting

There are two commercial composting collection methods presently in use in Linn and Benton Counties: self-haul to commercial composters and curbside collection.

9.10.1. Advantages and Disadvantages of Centralized Composting

Home composting is not practical for everyone. Curb side collection and recycling of yard debris is a sensible alternative for those who do not have the time or space to make compost. Centralized composting is also useful for processing materials that are difficult to handle at home, such as brush and woody prunings. The con-trolled high-temperature composting conditions at centralized facilities can assure a high-quality product from problem materials such as invasive weeds and diseased plants. A major disadvantage of centralized composting is the expense, effort, and environmental degradation of hauling raw materials to a central location for composting, then hauling material back in the form of finished compost.

9.10.2. Collection

Many methods are used to collect yard debris, offering varying levels of convenience and expense. Typically, there is a trade-off between the convenience of the collection system and its cost.

9.10.2.1. Self-Haul to a Compost Facility

Self-haul collection systems require individuals to take separated yard debris to a composting facility. Small fees are charged. Time and hauling costs can cut the savings in dumping fees for commercial landscapers if the facility is more than a few miles from a job site. Also, self haul systems require the use of a truck for large loads of yard debris. Linn and Benton County residents can self-haul compost to the Process and Recovery, PRC, located near the Coffin Butte Landfill.

9.10.2.2. Curbside Collection

Curbside collection of yard debris is the most convenient collection method for residents and the most effective in diverting large volumes of yard debris from the waste stream. It is also the most expensive. In Linn County, the curbside collection became available in the summer of 1993. Benton County began their program around the same time. Wheeled carts are provided for residents to de-posit yard debris. Only "clean" yard debris should be set out for collection. This includes the following:

- Grass clippings
- Leaves
- The brush which is in containers or bundled
- Small branches

In 2010, it became possible for Corvallis residents to include all food waste in their carts yard debris carts. no garbage, rocks, soil, or other non-organic materials are allowed. Plastic bags are not allowed in any curbside collection programs. They are difficult to remove and are a contaminant in the finished compost. "Biodegradable" plastic bags are not allowed either, as they are not all truly biodegradable and they complicate the processing of the material. Many communities promote the use of sturdy Kraft paper bags which are readily available and compost easily.

9.10.2.3. Commercial Compost Facilities

The collection system affects the design of a processing facility. The types and amounts of specific materials are some of the main factors considered. Commercial composting uses three major steps: preprocessing, active composting, and post-processing.

9.10.2.3.1 Preprocessing

Organic matter in Soil

Preprocessing begins with receiving, inspecting, and sorting the materials. Removing contaminants is important for making high-quality compost. Some contaminants like rocks, logs, or tire rims can seriously damage composting equipment. Sorting yard debris controls the materials that go directly to the composting area. This saves wear and tear on shredding equipment. Large materials are shredded to decrease break-down time. Many types of chipping and shredding equipment are available for size reduction.

9.10.2.3.2 Active Composting

In this phase, bacteria and other composting critters feast on the yard debris. Commercial processors can use a variety of methods and technologies some slow, some fast to break down the material. The methods vary in:

- Level of technology used
- Attention paid to managing and monitoring the operation
- Space required
- Length of time needed to obtain the finished product
- Ability to combine other organic materials with the yard debris.

Some processors use low-level technology, simply making huge piles of debris several stories tall or long windrows of material, letting everything compost slowly over one or two years. Low-level composting demands more space per volume of debris, but the savings in equipment and personnel costs may be substantial. The middle range of technology involves constructing and turning long windrows of decomposing materials. Windrow sizes vary widely but are typically five to ten feet wide, four to eight feet high, and hundreds of feet long. The equipment used to turn windrows ranges from front end loaders to specialized machinery de-signed exclusively for turning compost wind-rows. These operations create and maintain windows that will achieve high temperatures, allowing thermophilic bacteria to do the main composting work in as little as four to six weeks. Then the windrows are combined into large curing piles that are allowed to cool until the compost is stable, or mature. The highest levels of commercial composting technology employ composting digesters, computerized aeration and turning systems, and sophisticated odor control systems.

9.10.2.3.3 Postprocessing

Organic matter in Soil

Compost producers depend on a wide variety of end-users, or markets, for their compost, and they may tailor their postprocessing activities for particular users. Postprocessing activities prepare the finished compost for final use through screening, other grading methods, and packaging. Screening removes contaminants and uncomposted materials, including rocks, large wood chips, sticks, and large plastic items. Some operations, usually developed or heavily subsidized by municipalities, simply give their compost away to make room for the next batch. These operations do little or no postprocessing. More often, operations produce compost to compete in the soil products markets. The Department of Environmental Quality has regulations that apply to commercial composting operations. Local zoning and land-use laws cover the sitting of composting facilities. Composting operations may also be regulated by local air and water pollution agencies, which are concerned with dust, wastewater, and odors.

9.11 Home Composting

Composting at home is far more efficient than collecting and transporting organic materials to a centralized facility and then back to a home garden as a mulch or soil amendment. The best market for the finished product is right in one's back yard. Some people begin composting to cut down on the amount of waste in their garbage can. Others are motivated by a desire to use the compost produced. Composting is an excellent waste reduction technique because it keeps organic material out of the waste stream entirely. Compost improves the structure of the soil. The soil is easier to work, has good aeration and water retention characteristics, and increased resistance to erosion. Compost also helps hold elemental plant nutrients until plants are ready to use them. Soils improved by added compost are more likely to produce healthy plants able to resist disease and insect attacks.

9.11.1 Basic Compost Farming

Composting can be thought of as microorganism farming. Just as a good farmer keeps in mind the basics of soil, season, pests, and climate when growing a crop, a good composter focuses on the materials being composted and the climate around them to ensure a healthy compost crop. Almost any combination of yard wastes left out in the weather will decompose eventually. Understanding how to create the ideal conditions described here will help in making compost quickly and help to diagnose and solve composting problems.

9.11.1.1 Compost Materials

Anything organic leaves on the ground, a fallen tree, or a wood-framed house will decompose. The more resistant the material is to decay, however, the longer the process will take. Except in some special situations, decomposition is inevitable! A total absence of air, such as in a peat bog, will prevent decomposition. In very dry places, such as within the Antarctic, decomposition may be slowed. But everything organic that is out in the weather around Western Oregon will eventually become compost. Fallen leaves, grass clippings, sod stripped for a garden, weeds, squash vines, watermelon rinds even old cotton rags all come from once-living organisms and can be composted.

A diversity of materials is the key to a first-rate compost. In addition to the major plant nutrients such as nitrogen, phosphorus, and potassium, plants take up a host of minor and trace elements. The more diverse the materials composted, the more likely it is that these elements will be returned to the plants. This does not mean that the materials will compost more quickly or more thoroughly, but that they will feed the plants better.

Table – 9.1: Common Compostable Organic Waste Resources

Glass clippings	Landscapers are always trying to get rid of them.
Yard Wastes	Weeds, old plants, wilted flowers
Leaves	You'll find these bagged and waiting at neighbors' curbside.
Food scraps	Except for bread, meat, fat, bones, dairy, or oily foods. They must be buried under 8" of soil, composted by earthworms, or in a hot compost pile.
Wood Chips	A tree service will deliver a load if you are willing to take a large quantity. Use first on garden paths, then compost it after the initial decay has begun.
Sawdust	This is best if first used as a livestock litter or allowed to weather since it takes a lot of nitrogen to break it down.
Seaweed	Found washed up on some beaches. It's an excellent source of many plant nutrients
Hair	Very high in nitrogen. Rescue some from the garbage at barbershops and beauty parlors.
Coffee grounds and filters	Almost every home and office has coffee grounds. Coffee chaff is a beautiful mulch. Available from coffee roasters.
Manures	Rabbit, cow, and goat manures are the only sterile manures to use. These manures provide useful organisms.

9.11.1.2. Non-Compostable Organic Materials

Organic matter in Soil

Everything that was once alive will compost. However, not everything belongs in a compost pile. Some materials that create problems and should be kept out of home compost systems are listed in Table – 9.2.

Table – 9.2: Non-Compostable Organic Waste

Do **NOT** compost these materials:

Plants infected with disease or a severe insect attack where eggs could be preserved or where the insects them-selves could survive despite the compost pile's heat (examples are apple scab, aphids, and tent caterpillars).

Ivy, succulents, and certain pernicious weeds such as morning glory and buttercups; and **grasses spread by rhizomes** such as quack grass. These may not be killed by the heat of decomposition and can choke out other plants when compost is used in the garden.

Cat, dog, and bird manures, which contain pathogens harmful to children. These pathogens are not always killed in the heat of the compost pile.

Meat and fish leftovers, bones, or greasy fatty foods such as oils, butter, and cheeses.

Piles made entirely of waxy leaves such as are hidden-dron and English Laurel, or pine needles break down very slowly. Try composting small amounts of these mixed with other materials, shred them first or use them as mulch.

9.11.1.3 Managing Animal Wastes

The only acceptable ways to dispose of cat and dog feces is to flush them down the toilet or bury them in the ornamental areas of the garden. Pet wastes should not be composted with food or yard wastes. Dog, cat, and bird feces can carry pathogens that are dangerous to people, so they should be handled as little as possible. These wastes should be buried in ornamental garden areas only, where they will be undisturbed for at least two years. Pet wastes should not be buried within 100 feet of domestic water well, lake, or stream. A pit 2- to 3-feet deep, covered securely with a heavy board, can serve as a burial area for one or two pets over an extended period. A little soil, sawdust, peat moss, or compost should be thrown on top of each deposit. When the hole is filled to within 1 foot of the surface, it should be filled with soil and a new pet should be started. Burial is only recommended for small amounts of pet wastes.

9.11.2 Composting Systems

9.11.2.1 The Basics

The basic components necessary for composting are air, water, and food. The process of composting can be as simple or as complex as one wants to make it. Passive composting can be simply making a pile of materials and letting them break down slowly. Active composting involves paying attention to the amounts and types of materials and turning the pile frequently. There are three crucial components to composting. To live, the microorganisms that make decomposition happen need the same basic things as humans-oxygen, water, and nutritious food. Turning or mixing the compost occasionally will get oxygen into the pile. While the microorganisms need water, if they have too much water, they will drown. A good rule of thumb is that compost should be as wet as a wrung-out rag. And lastly, those microorganisms need the right nutrients in their food. Most things composted are either brown or green. Brown material, like fallen leaves, are very high in carbon. Green materials are a rich nitrogen source. A healthy compost pile needs both types of materials. Microorganisms need 30 times more carbon than nitrogen so adding more brown materials makes a compost pile function best. A more in-depth discussion of the science of composting is included later in this chapter.

9.11.2.2 Criteria for Selecting a Compost System

There are many ways to make compost. Home compost methods range from mulched paths that are replenished every other year, to turning units that are maintained weekly. Many compost systems can be built with scavenged materials, some require nothing but the soil in a garden, and others cost over $300. Composting systems are organized by the type of wastes they process: yard wastes are composted by using them as mulches or in holding and turning units; vegetative kitchen food wastes are composted either through soil incorporation or in worm bins. Turning units also may be used to compost kitchen and yard waste together in a hot pile for those willing to turn the piles regularly. Usually, food wastes should be composted in closed systems separately from yard wastes to keep rodents and other pests from becoming a problem in the open, longer-standing yard waste composting systems. Yard wastes are generally not susceptible to pest problems, so they may be composted in a variety of open systems. The style depends on what materials are to be recycled, how much space is available, when com-post is needed, and what it will be used for.

9.11.2.3 Composting Yard Wastes

Yard wastes can be composted in simple holding units where they will sit undisturbed bed for slow decomposition, in turning bins that produce finished compost in as little as a month, or as mulches on paths or around planting until they decompose in a year or two. Holding units are simple container s used to store yard and garden waste in an organized way until the materials break down. Using a holding unit is the easiest way to compost. It requires no turning or other labor except placing wastes into a pile or bin as they are generated. Non-woody materials such as grass clippings, garden weeds, crop wastes, and leaves work best in these systems. Decomposition can take from six months to two years. However, the process can be sped up by chopping or shredding wastes, mixing green and brown materials, and maintaining proper moisture. Since materials are continuously added to holding units, they are at various stages of decomposition. Generally, the more finished compost is at the bottom of the pile, while partially decomposed materials are near the top. Once it is determined that the finished compost is at the bottom of a holding bin or pile, the compost is ready to be harvested and used (Finished compost is somewhat of personal judgment. It should look like mulch, have a nice earthy smell, and not be changing very much). To harvest the compost, the holding unit is removed from the compost pile and placed next to it. Yard wastes are then forked from the top of the old pile into the bottom of the empty holding unit until rich compost is found. The compost can be used and the holding unit is ready to receive additional yard wastes. Holding units can be made of light materials so they may be easily taken apart and moved around the garden. Some examples of holding units include circles of snow fencing or hardware cloth, old wooden pallets lashed together, or wireframed in wood. More permanent holding areas can be made by stacking cinder blocks or mortaring bricks or rocks together. It is helpful to have two of these stationary bins, one to use for fresh wastes while the other is curing. Sod also can be composted in a holding system, with or without a structure. Simply pile freshly stripped sod roots up, grass down. Make sure it is thoroughly wet, and cover with black plastic to keep light out. Sod takes one to three years to decompose completely. Decomposition of sod piles can be shortened to as little as six months by adding a high-nitrogen fertilizer such as cottonseed meal or ammonium sulfate. Covered piles are also an effective way to kill quack grass and some other noxious weeds.

9.11.2.3.1 Turning Units

Turning units are typically a series of bins used for building and turning hot compost piles. An alternative turning system is a horizontally mounted rotation barrel. A turning unit allows wastes to be conveniently mixed for regular aeration. This speeds composting by providing bacteria with the air they need to break down materials. Turning systems require frequent maintenance and involve preparation of the wastes to be composted. These units can be expensive to buy or build. However, the effort and expense are rewarded with large quantities of compost produced in a short time. Non-woody yard wastes, along with vegetable wastes from the kitchen, maybe composted in turning units. Composting in these units is most efficiently done in batches. Materials should be stockpiled until enough are on hand to make a pile that fills a 3 ft. by 3 ft. by 3 ft. bin, or almost fills a barrel composter. (To reduce odors and pests, food wastes should be stored in a sealed container until enough materials are available to make a large pile).

- Gather all the materials needed to make a pile that is at least 3 cubic feet. Use both green and brown materials to approximate the 30:1 carbon to nitrogen balance. Increase the decomposition rate of the materials by running them through a shredder or chop them with a spade or machete on a piece of plywood. Brown leaves may be run over with a rotary lawn mower to break them down.

- Start building the pile with a 4- to the 6-inch base of brown material. If the pile is going to sit for a few weeks or more, use coarse material (small branches, corn stalks, straw) for this base layer to let air into the pile. Moisten materials.

- Next, add a 4- to 6-inch layer of green materials. If the greens are not very fresh, sprinkle on a small amount of blood meal or cottonseed meal, poultry manure, or another high-nitrogen source. Fresh grass clippings should be used in thin layers. Mix the green and brown layers so bacteria can feed on both simultaneously.

- These piles should be monitored and turned after temperatures have peaked and begun to fall, in 4 to 7 days; then turned a second time when the temperature peaks again, 4 to 7 days later. Com-post processed this way will be ready in 3 weeks. Rotating barrel units do not need layering; mate-rial can be thrown in and mixed up. If rotating barrel composters are turned every 2 to 4 days, compost will be ready to use in 2 to 3 weeks.

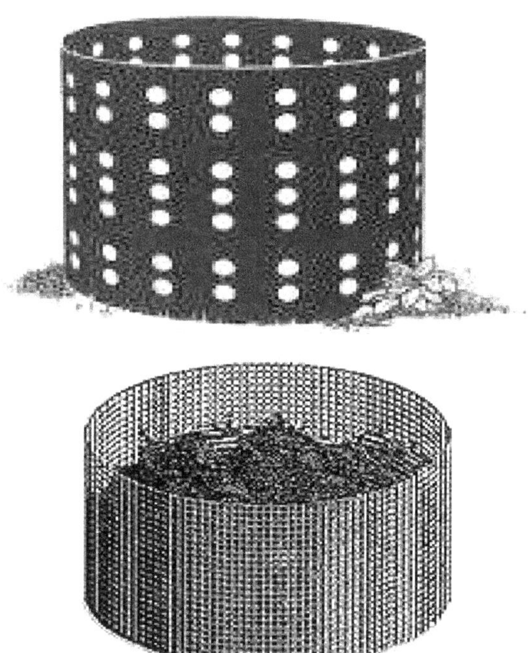

Figure – 9.1: Holding units such as these are easy to set up. The wire enclosure can be made by using a large loop of chicken wire, snow fence, or Aquamesh. To empty the bin, it is simply dismantled.

A rotating barrel composter may be made from a 55-gallon drum with a loading door cut and hinged. Aeration holes must be cut at the ends or around the barrel. A variety of rotating barrel composters is available commercially. Avoid barrel units made entirely from metal perforated with 1" holes, as they leave materials dry or clumped together. Ideally, barrel units should have flat sides, or "fins" inside to lift and drop materials as the barrel is turned.

9.11.2.3.2 Mulches

Mulches are organic materials spread over the surface of the soil to suppress weeds, keep plant roots cool and moist, and prevent soil from eroding or compacting. Mulches are used around plants in the garden, or as a soft "paving" for paths and play areas. An ideal mulch material is one that costs nothing, is easy to keep in place, and reduces evaporation of soil moisture while permitting rapid penetration of water. There is a great variety of organic and inorganic materials that can be used for mulching. In this manual, only organic mulches will be discussed. Some common organic materials used for mulches include wood chips, lawn clippings, compost, sawdust, leaves from deciduous trees and shrubs, manure, and pine needles. It is also possible to mulch with commercial by-products such as coffee chaff and buckwheat hulls, or straw. The focus here will be on using organic wastes that are readily available in and around our homes.

Organic matter in Soil

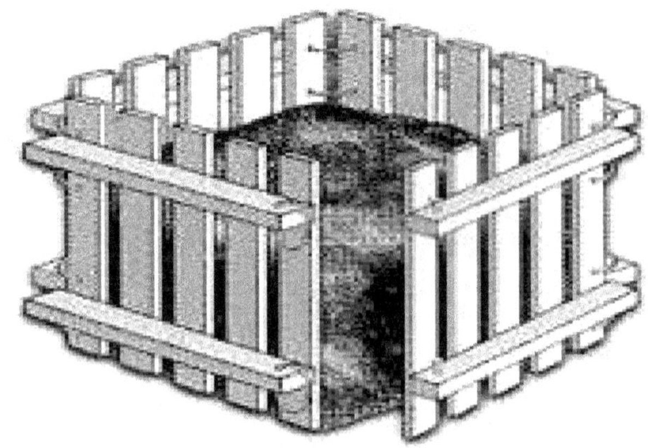

Figure – 9.2: Bins built from used pallets also help to keep those pallets out of the waste stream and are a preferred bin type for hard-core recyclers. By simply building a swinging gate with the front pallet, it serves well as a turning unit

These materials are suitable for surface mulching around trees, shrubs, and other perennial plantings. However, in annual flower and vegetable gardens, it is best to mulch with non-woody materials such as lawn clippings, compost, and other green garden trimmings. Non-woody materials break down quickly and can then be turned under without competing with plants for the nitrogen that bacteria need to break down woody wastes. If woody wastes are used in an annual garden, they should be pulled aside before tilling so that they do not use up nitrogen that plants need. If woody wastes are tilled in, they must be balanced by adding a high-nitrogen source such as blood meal. The material most commonly used for mulching commercial landscaping is ground bark ("beauty bark"). A more natural-looking alternative is the chipped waste from tree pruning and removal operations. This material can often be obtained for free by calling a tree service. If one has tree work done at home, the tree service may be willing to leave the chips. Any leaves left with the branches will decompose in a short time, adding to the beauty of the variegated mulch. Wood chip makes an excellent path and plays area material, as it decomposes slowly and softens the surface.

9.11.3 Composting Food

Non-fatty food wastes may be composted by incorporating them into the soil where they will break down to fertilize established or future plantings, by placing them in worm bins that produce high quality "castings" for use on plants indoors or out or layering them in hot piles along with yard wastes as described in the previous section. Food wastes incorporated into the soil can take from one month to one year to decompose fully. It takes worms three to six months to transform a bin of wastes into vermicompost. Hot piles can compost a mixed load of food and yard wastes in three weeks.

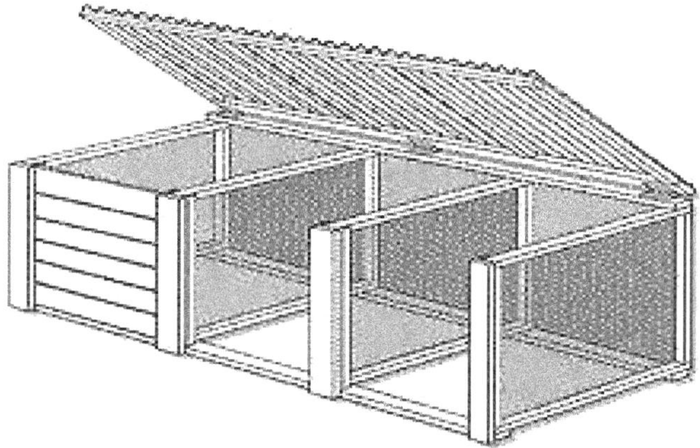

Figure – 9.3: Bin turning unit. For the most de-manding waste volumes, this type of unit allows for multi-stage composting. Fresh material is added to one bin, then turned and shoveled into the next bin. The finished compost is removed from the final bin.

9.11.3.1 Soil incorporation

Soil incorporation is the simplest method for composting food waste. A hole is dug one foot deep, and the food wastes are chopped and mixed into the soil, then covered with at least 8 inches of additional soil. (Pet wastes can also be buried in the soil as long as it is done in ornamental gardens, not vegetable gardens). Depending on soil temperature, the number of micro-organisms in the soil, and the carbon content of the wastes, decomposition will occur in one month to one year. Food wastes such as meat, bones, or fatty foods such as cheese and salad dressing are not recommended for soil in-corporation. These foods have the potential of attracting rodents, dogs, cats, or flies.

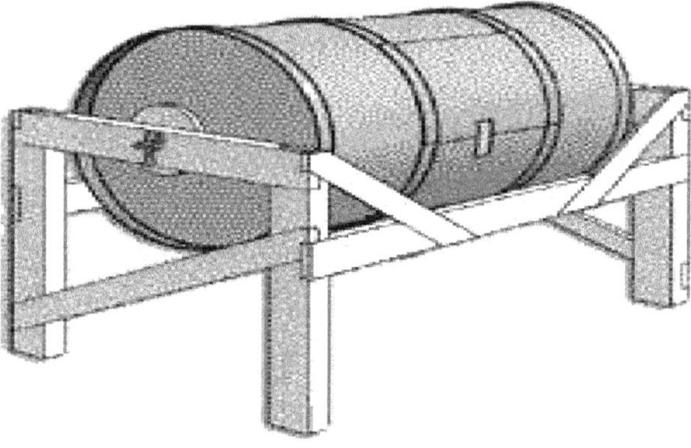

Figure – 9.4: Rotating barrel bin. Although more challenging to build, the enclosed bin can help where pests are a problem. Aeration is provided by simply rotating the barrel, which is easier than having to fetch a shovel or pitchfork.

Food wastes can be incorporated around the drip line of trees or shrubs by using a post hole digger or shovel. The tree roots actively feed in this zone and will benefit most from nutrients added there. Food wastes also may be buried in a fallow area of an annual garden, or a trench may be dug and filled with soil as food waste is added. In English gardens, a form of soil incorporation known as "pit and trench" composting is practiced. This is a simple three-year rotation of soil incorporation of kitchen wastes, growing crops, and path making. In the first season, a trench is dug, filled with food wastes, and covered. At the same time, another row is used to grow crops and a third is used as a path. In the second year, the fertile soil of the former compost trench is used to grow crops, the former crop row is used as a path, and the path is dug as a new trench. After the third year of rotation, the cycle starts over. This form of composting keeps the garden perpetually fertile with a small organizational effort.

9.11.3.2 Anaerobic composters

Table – 9.3: Compostable Food Wastes

Can Be Composted	Can Not Be Composted
Apples	Butter
Apple peels	Bones
Cabbage	Cheese
Carrots	Chicken
Celery	Fish scraps
Coffee grounds/filters	Lard
Eggshells	Mayonnaise
Grapefruit	Meat scraps
Lettuce	Milk
Onion peel	Peanut butter
Orange peel	Sour cream
Pears	Vegetable oil
Pineapple	Yogurt
Potatoes	
Pumpkin shell	
Squash	
Tea leaves and bags	
Tomatoes	
Turnip leaves	

Anaerobic composters, such as the Gedye bin, can also be used to decompose both food and yard waste. In anaerobic composting, bacteria break down the organic material without the addition of oxygen. This type of composting retains more nitrogen while producing methane but does not reach temperatures high enough to kill weed seeds or pathogens. Anaerobic systems usually consist of a closed bin or dark plastic bag which is filled with vegetative waste, moistened, closed, and placed

in the sun for 10 to 12 weeks. To avoid animal pests it is best to cover the bottom of the composting bin with wire mesh.

9.11.3.3 Hot compost piles

Hot compost piles are the only safe way to compost food and yard wastes together without pest problems. They are also the best way to kill soil diseases and weed seeds in compost and to produce compost in a short period. Not everyone wants or needs to make hot compost piles. Here is a recipe for those who do: Gather all the materials needed to make a pile that is at least 3 cubic feet. Use both green and brown materials to approximate the 30:1 carbon to nitrogen balance.

- To increase the decomposition rate of the materials, run them through a shredder, or chop them with a spade or machete on a piece of plywood. Brown leaves may be run over with a rotary lawn mower to break them down.
- Start building the pile with a 4- to the 6-inch base of brown material. If the pile is going to sit for a few weeks or more, use coarse material (small branches, corn stalks, straw) for this base layer to let air into the pile. Moisten materials.
- Next, add a 4- to 6-inch layer of green materials. If the greens are not very fresh, sprinkle on a small amount of blood meal or cottonseed meal, poultry manure, or another high-nitrogen source. Fresh grass clippings should be used in thin layers. Mix the green and brown layers so bacteria can feed on both simultaneously.
- Continue alternating and mixing layers of green and brown materials, adding water and extra green materials as needed, until the pile is 3 to 4 feet high (fill the bin).
- Close bin or cover pile and wait.
- Monitor temperature in the interior of the pile regularly. It should peak between 120° to 160° F in 5 to 10 days.
- When the temperature begins to decrease, turn the pile. Take materials from the outer edges and top off the pile and place them at the base and middle of the new pile. Those from the middle should be on the outside edges and top of the new pile.
- Continue monitoring the temperature in the pile.
- About one week later, the temperature of the pile should peak. Turn the pile again. After another week, the compost should be finished. Piles made this way without food wastes do not need to be turned; they will be finished in 3 to 4 months.

Organic matter in Soil

9.11.3.4 Vermicomposting

Vermicomposting (worm bin composition) uses red worms in an enclosed container to convert vegetable and fruit scraps into a nutrient-rich soil amendment called worm castings. The materials used are

- Container
- Bedding
- Red worms
- Kitchen scraps

9.11.3.4.1 Container

The size of the container depends on the amount of waste to be composted. A worm bin can be made by using almost any container that is an appropriate size, prevents light from entering, has air vents, and is covered. The surface area is more important than depth for a worm system. Generally, one square foot of surface is required for every pound of food waste to be composted per week.

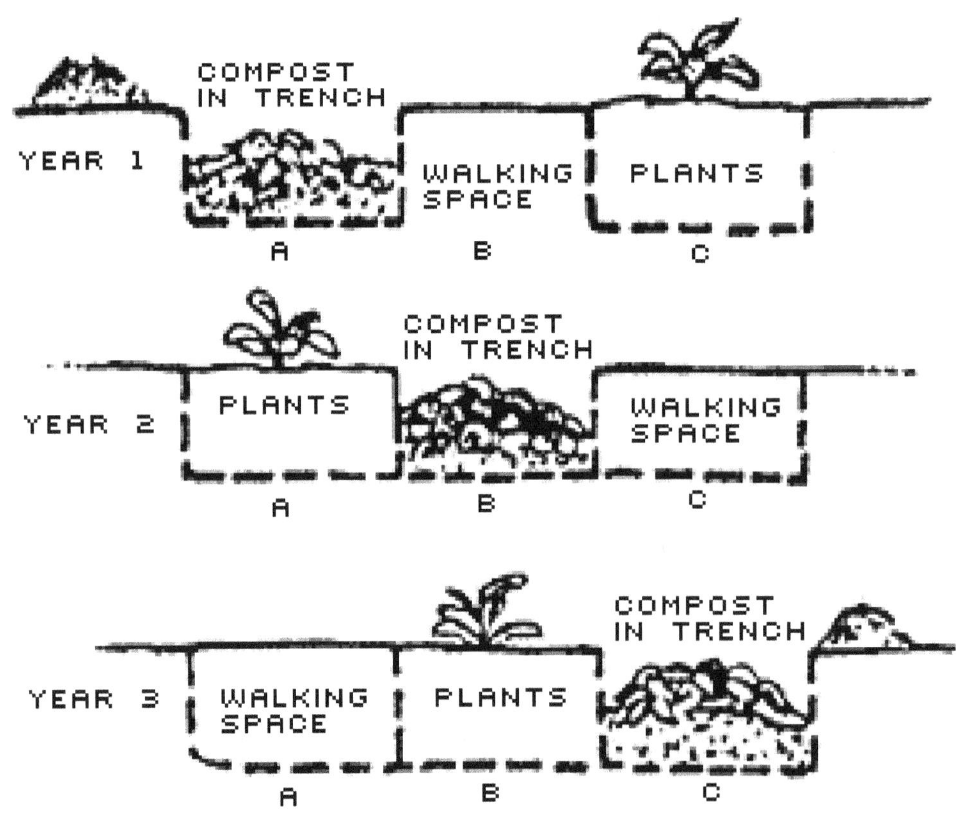

9.11.3.4.2 Bedding

Suitable bedding materials include shredded newspaper or cardboard, dry leaves, straw, peat moss, and wood shavings.

9.11.3.4.3 Redworms

The most popular redworm used for vermicomposting is *Eisenia fetida*. In nature, redworms are surface dwellers that live in the top layer of soil under the organic debris that is their food. By creating suitable living conditions, one can take advantage of the redworm's ability to recycle organic matter. Worms eat half their weight in food scraps and about an equal amount of bedding each day. A bin that starts with about a 1 pound of worms will need to be fed a handful of food every other day. As worms multiply the food supply should be increased.

Figure – 9.6: Redworms

Table – 9.4: Fun Facts About Worms

- There are more than 3,500 species of earthworms worldwide, including red worms.
- Each worm has five pairs of hearts and a simple brain.
- The average worm is made up of 100 to 200 ringed segments.
- A worm can grow a new head or tail if some of its segments are nipped off.
- Worms have no teeth or eyes but have highly sensitive skin.
- Worms breathe through their skin.
- A worm can eat about half its weight in food scraps every day.
- An enlarged cummerbund-like band near the worm's head holds the

Organic matter in Soil

> reproductive organs.
> - Each worm is both male and female (hermaphroditic).
> - Worms exchange sperm to reproduce and each produces an egg (cocoon) from which 2 to 4 baby worms emerge.
> - Eight breeding worms can become 1,500 worms in 6 months.
> - Each healthy worm may produce an egg capsule every 7 to 10 days. These capsules incubate for 14 to 21 days.
> - The baby worms will mature to breeding age in 2 to 3 months.
> - A healthy redworm can live from 7 to 10 years and grows to about 3 inches.

Source: *City of Eugene Solid Waste & Recycling Program and OSU Lane County Extension Service*

9.11.3.4.4 Kitchen scraps

Redworms are capable of eating most kitchen scraps, but some waste is better left out of the bin to avoid odor or pest problems. Do not compost meats, fish, dairy products, oily foods, or cat and dog waste. Foods that can be added to the worm bin include:

- Vegetable scraps
- Fruit peels or pulp
- Coffee and tea grounds and filters
- Pieces of bread (without butter or mayonnaise)

Food may be cut up or ground into small pieces to speed up the process. This provides more surface area for the worms to feed on. Worm bins are fun and an interesting way to compost non-fatty kitchen wastes. Also, they compost the newsprint, cardboard, or other wastes used as bedding. Worm bins are most efficient if sized and stocked according to the amount of waste to be handled. Mary Appelhof's book "Worms Eat My Garbage" provides information on how to determine what size a worm bin should be and the amount of bedding and worms required for an efficient system. Another source of information on worms and worm composting is the "Worm Digest."

9.11.4. Compost Uses

Compost is a much-needed resource. It is not only useful to the home gardener but is essential to the restoration of landscapes where topsoil has been removed or destroyed during construction or mining operations. Compost is increasingly being applied to agricultural and forest lands that have been depleted of

Organic matter in Soil

their organic matter. The most common use of compost today is probably in topsoil mixes used in the landscape industry.

9.11.4.1. Compost is typically applied

a) To mulch or "top dress" planted trees.
b) To amend the soil before planting.
c) To amend potting mixes.

9.11.4.1.1. Mulching

Gardeners and landscapers use mulches and top dressings over the surface of the soil to suppress weeds, keep plant roots cool and moist, conserve water, maintain a loose and porous surface, and prevent soil from eroding or compacting. Com-post also gives plantings an attractive, natural appearance. Compost can be used to mulch around flower and vegetable plants, shrubs, trees, and ground covers. To prepare an area for mulching, first clear away any visible grass or weeds that might grow up through the mulch. Make sure to remove the roots of any weedy plants that spread vegetative, such as quack grass, ivy, and buttercup. Different types of plants benefit from varying application rates and grades of mulch. Recommended uses of compost as mulch and top dressings are shown in Table – 9.5.

Table – 9.5: Using compost as Mulch

On Flower and Vegetable Beds:
- Screen or pick through compost to remove large, woody material. They are less attractive and will compete for nitrogen if mixed into the soil.
- Apply ½ to 1 inch of compost over the entire bed, or place in rings around each plant ex-tending as far as the outermost leaves. Always keep mulches a few inches away from the base of the plant to prevent damage by pests and disease.

On Lawns:
- Use screened commercial compost, or sift homemade compost through a ½ inch or finer mesh. Mix with an equal amount of sand or sandy soil.
- Spread compost/sand mix in ¼ to ½ inch lay-ers after thatching or coring and before re-seeding.

On Trees and Shrubs:
- Remove the sod from around trees and shrubs as far as branches spread. If this is impractical, remove sod in a circle a minimum of 4 feet in diameter around plants.
- Use coarse compost or material left after sift-ing. Remove only the largest branches and rocks.

For Erosion Control:
- Spread coarse compost, or materials left after sifting, in 2- to 4-inch deep layers

over the entire planting area or in rings extending to the drip line.

- Mulch exposed slopes or erosion-prone areas with 2 to 4 inches of coarse compost.

9.11.4.1.2 Soil Amendment

Compost can be used to enrich garden soils before planting annuals, ground covers, shrubs, and trees. Many commercial topsoil mixes contain composted yard debris or sewage sludge as a major component. This may be mixed with sand, sandy soil removed from construction sites, peat moss, and/or ground bark. Soils may be amended by mixing compost top-soil mixes with the existing soil. If a rich compost or topsoil mix is laid on top of the existing soil without mixing, the zone where they meet can become a barrier to roots and water. In this condition, plants often develop shallow roots and eventually blow over or suffer from a lack of water and nutrients. Recommended applications for different situations are shown in Table – 9.6.

Table – 9.6: Using Compost as Soil Amendment

In Flower and Vegetable Beds and Ground Covers:
- Dig or till base soil to a minimum depth of 8- 10 inches.
- Mix 3 to 4 inches of compost through the entire depth. For poor soils, mix an additional 3 inches of compost into the top 3 inches of amended soil. In established gardens, mix 2 to 4 inches of compost into the top 6 to 10 inches of soil each year before planting.

On Lawns:
- Till base soil to a depth of 6 inches.
- Mix 4 inches of fine-textured compost into the loosened base soil.

Planting Trees and Shrubs:
- Dig or till base soil to a minimum depth of 8 to 10 inches throughout the planting area, or an area 2 to 5 times the width of the root ball of individual specimens.
- Mix 3 to 4 inches of compost through the entire depth. For poor soils, mix an additional 3 inches of compost into the amended topsoil.
- Do not use compost at the bottom of the individual planting holes or to fill the holes. Mulch the surface with wood chips or coarse compost.

9.11.4.1.3 Potting and Seedling Mixes

Sifted compost can be used to make a rich, loose potting soil for patio planters, house plants, or for starting seedlings in flats. Compost can be used to enrich purchased potting mixes or to make mixes at home. Plants growing in containers are entirely reliant on the water and nutrients that are provided in the potting mix. Compost is excellent for container growing mixes because it stores moisture effectively and provides a variety of nutrients not typically supplied in

Organic matter in Soil

commercial fertilizers or soil-free potting mixes. However, because of the limits of the container, it is essential to amend compost-based potting mixes with a "complete" fertilizer to provide an adequate supply of macronutrients (N-P-K). Simple "recipes" for making your compost mixes are shown in Table – 9.7.

Table – 9.7: Using Compost in Potting mixes

For Starting and Growing Seedlings in Flats or Small Containers
• Sift compost through a mesh ½ inch or finer.
• Mix 2 parts sifted compost, 1 part coarse sand, and 1 part Sphagnum peat moss. Add ½ cup of lime for each bushel (8 gallons) of the total mix. Use liquid fertilizers when true leaves emerge.
For Growing Transplants and Plants in Larger Containers
• Sift compost through a 1-inch mesh or remove larger particles by hand. Mix 2 parts compost, 1 part ground bark, perlite, or pumice, 1 part coarse sand, and 1 part loamy soil or peat moss. Add ½ cup of lime and ½ cup of 10-10-10 fertilizer for each bushel (8 gallons) of the mix. (An organic fertilizer alternative can be made from ½ cup blood meal or cotton-seed meal, 1 cup of rock phosphate, and ½ cup of kelp meal.)

9.12 Troubleshooting

The troubleshooting chart, Table – 9.8 is based on information found in the book Home Com-posting Made Easy by C. Forrest McDowell and Tricia Clark-McDowell, and The Incredible Heap: A Guide to Compost Gardening by Stu Campbell.

Table – 9.8: Troubleshooting Compost Piles

Problem	Symptom/Cause	Solution
The compost pile does not heat up	Too Wet: compost materials are soggy; not enough air.	Turn the pile, adding dry absorbent material (carbon or "brown") like straw or corn stalks
	Too Dry: not enough moisture	Moisten pile without saturating it.
	The pile is damp and warm right in the middle, but nowhere else. Pile is not decomposing.	Turn pile, adding nitrogen-rich materials such as manure, grass clippings, fresh leaves, or vegetable or fruit wastes.

Organic matter in Soil

Ammonia smell	Too much nitrogen (green matter such as grass clippings) in the pile or the pile is too alkaline (possibly too much limestone added).	If nitrogen problem: turn the pile and add more carbon (brown) material. If alkaline related: turn the pile and add acid material like sawdust, oak leaves, or vegetable scraps.
"Rotten Egg" smell	The pile is too wet and there isn't enough oxygen.	Turn pile to aerate it and add dry carbon (brown) materials to absorb excessive moisture
The center is dry and contains tough, woody wastes.	Not enough water in the pile. Too much woody material.	Turn and moisten; add fresh green wastes; chop or shred.
Pests (rats, raccoons, fruit flies, etc.)	Rodents and raccoons are attracted to meat and fatty food scraps like cheese and other dairy products.	Remove meat/fatty foods from the pile. Turn pile to increase temperature. Balance carbon to nitrogen ratio. Use rodent-proof bin; keep a lid on, put $\frac{1}{4}$-inch wire mesh on bottom or sides, and insure air venting holes are less than the $\frac{1}{2}$-inch diameter.
	Flies, gnats, etc. are attracted to uncovered wastes, especially fruits, melons, and vegetables.	Don't leave exposed! Mix or cover with carbon (brown) materials, finished compost, or some soil.
The pile is damp and sweet-smelling, but will not heat up.	Lack of nitrogen in pile. The compost is done!	Mix in fresh grass clippings or nitrogen fertilizer.

9.13 Composting Works

Technical Information Chemical and biological factors affect the decomposition of organic materials.

9.13.1 The Life Cycle of a Heap

The decomposition and recombining of various forms of plant and animal life (organic matter) create compost. Inseparable from these dead residues are the living

microorganisms that decompose or digest them. The length of the process depends on several factors: density of the material, amount of surface area exposed, the balance of carbon and nitrogen, and environmental conditions such as moisture, air, and temperature. These factors, in various combinations, set the stage for the cast of characters bacteria, fungi, millipedes, earthworms, and other living inhabitants of the compost pile and determine the speed at which these characters perform.

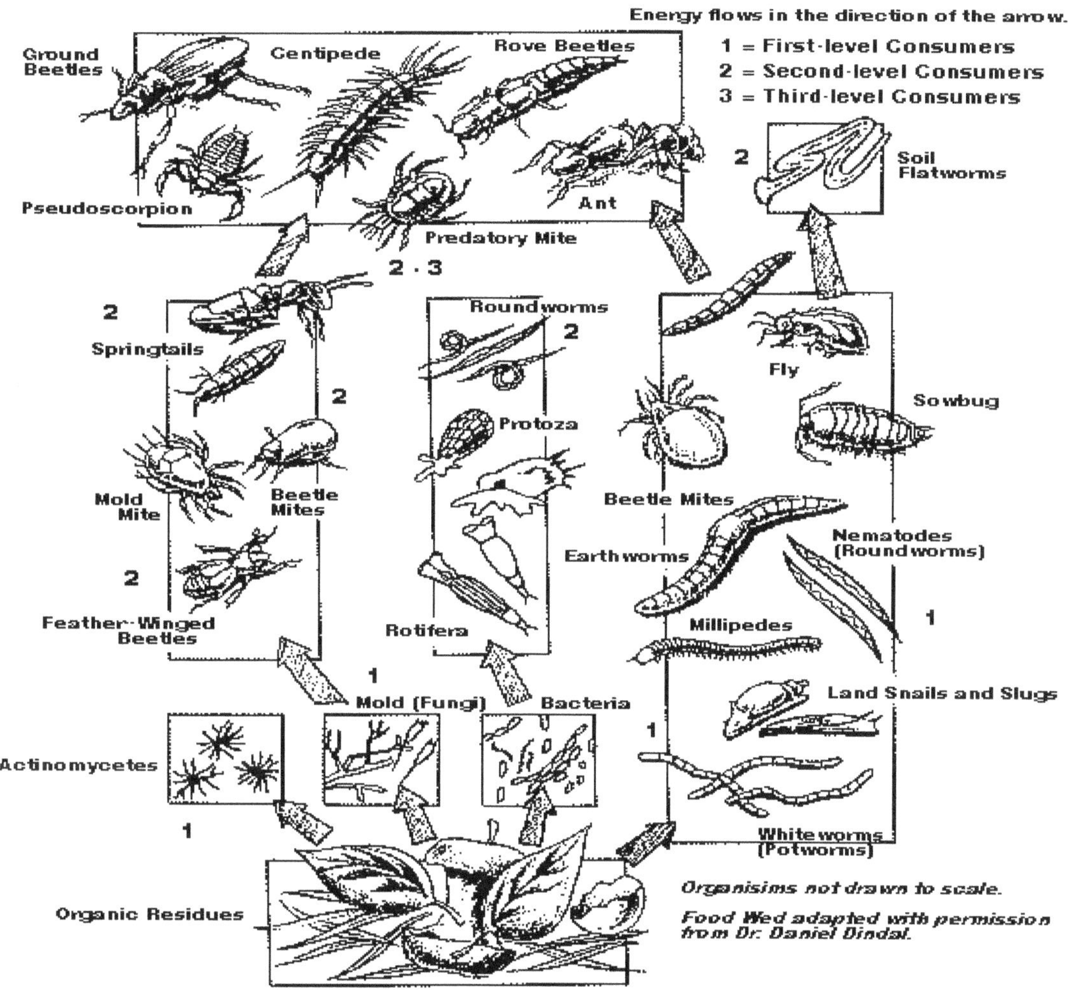

Figure – 9.5: Food web at the compost pile. (Source: The Ecology of Compost, Daniel Dindal)

The process of decomposition is a very complex but natural one. Many organisms are responsible for the breakdown of organic matter. Although most are not seen by the human eye, they are there throughout the process. Others that are large enough to see are usually associated with the later breakdown stages. Not all bugs are bad. All bugs play a role in nature. Many compost pile organisms eat other

organisms and turn them into compost. At least one-third of the volume in a compost pile is made up of the dead, decomposed bodies of soil organisms. Still, a compost pile shouldn't allow in any old bugs. First-time composters may be surprised by the size and complexity of the community of small organisms residing in a compost pile. These organisms, which include many insects, bugs, slugs, bacteria, and fungi, form what is called a "food web" (Figure – 9.5).

In the food web, each organism has a job to do in turning organic waste into dark, crumbly finished compost. The food web decomposition process includes:
- Level One - primary consumers. Organisms that shred organic matter and the microscopic organisms that eat the shredded organic residues.
- Level Two - secondary consumers. Organ-isms that eat level one organism.
- Level Three - tertiary consumers. Organisms that eat level two organisms.

All members of the compost food web are very beneficial to a compost pile and should be left alone to do their work. They need each other to survive. If any of the member organisms are removed by using insecticides, their natural cycle is disrupted and the compost is contaminated with insecticide residues.

9.13.1.1. Level One - Primary Consumers

This level is made up of herbivores: bacteria, fungi, Actinomycetes, nematodes, mites, snails, slugs, earthworms, millipedes, sowbugs, and worms. Note that some types of mites are carnivores. The most productive members of a compost pile's food web are the bacteria, which are chemical decomposers. As a group, they can eat nearly anything. Some are so adaptable that they can use more than a hundred different organic compounds as their source of carbon due to their ability to produce a variety of enzymes. Usually, they can produce the appropriate enzyme to digest whatever material they find themselves on. Every piece of organic matter placed in the pile is covered with varying amounts of bacteria. As they digest the organic material and break it down into its basic elements, they are also reproducing at an incredible rate. One gram of bacteria can become about 450 grams of bacteria in only three hours. There are many kinds of specialized bacteria operating in different temperature ranges.

9.13.1.1.1. Psychrophilic

Psychrophilic bacteria work best in temperatures of about 55 degrees F but can stay on the job even in near-freezing conditions. This is why a compost pile sinks in the winter; these bacteria are busy breaking down organic matter. As these cooler

Organic matter in Soil

bacteria go to work, their activity begins to heat the pile. The increased temperature creates the ideal conditions for the next type of bacteria to arrive.

9.13.1.1.2 Mesophilic

Mesophilic bacteria work best in temperatures of about 70 degrees F to 90 degrees F but can stay on the job in even hotter conditions. The activity of mesophilic bacteria can heat the pile to temperatures greater than 110 degrees F.

9.13.1.1.3 Thermophilic

Thermophilic bacteria become active when the temperature reaches between 104 degrees F to 200 degrees F. If a compost pile steams in the morning or on a frosty day, it's because these bacteria are busy at work decomposing the organic waste. These bacteria generally last for up to five days and then the pile begins to cool. As the psychrophiles eat away at the organic matter, they give off a small amount of heat. If conditions are right for rapid growth, this heat will be sufficient to set the stage for the mesophiles. In many compost piles, these efficient mid-range bacteria do most of the work. However, given optimal conditions, they may produce enough heat to kick in the real hotshots–the thermophiles. Although at first, they are the most active decomposers, the bacteria are not alone in all of this work. Other microbes, fungi, and a host of in-vertebrate decomposers also take part. Some are active in the heating cycle, but most other organisms prefer the cooler temperatures of later de-composition. After temperatures go down, the decomposing pile becomes a real zoo. Larger organisms, many of them feeding on the piles' earlier inhabitants, add diversity to the action.

9.13.1.1.4 Actinomycetes

Actinomycetes produce grayish cobwebby growths (molds) throughout the compost that give the pile a pleasing, earthy smell, similar to a rotting log. They are frequently seen in drier parts of the pile and survive a wide range of temperatures.

9.13.1.1.5 Fungi

Fungi send their thin mycelial fibers out far from their spore-forming reproductive bodies. Molds are a form of fungi. The presence of mold and fungi usually implies decay. The most common of these pop up on a cool pile. Fungal decomposition is less efficient than bacterial decay as cold temperatures greatly restrict its growth. Snails, slugs, millipedes, sowbugs, pillbugs, mites, and earthworms are the larger invertebrates that shred the plant materials, creating more surface area for action by the microscopic fungi, bacteria, and actinomycetes, which

are in turn eaten by organisms such as mites and springtails. These creatures all excrete "castings" that are very dark and fine, and great for your plants.

9.13.1.1.6 Snails

Snails are terrestrial mollusks, typically having a spirally coiled shell, broad retractile foot, and distinct head. They generally feed on living plant material but will attack fresh garbage and plant debris.

9.13.1.1.7 Slugs

Slugs are snails without the shell. They too feed on living plant material, fresh garbage, and plant debris, and will also show up in the compost heap.

9.13.1.1.8 Millipedes

Millipedes are non-poisonous arthropods with cylindrical bodies of 20 to 100 segments, with two pairs of legs per segment. They feed mainly on decaying plant tissue but will also eat insect carcasses and excrement.

9.13.1.1.9 Sow Bugs

Sow Bugs are fat-bodied crustaceans with delicate plate-like gills along the lower surface of their abdomens which must be kept moist. They move slowly and feed on rot-ting woody materials and highly durable leaf tissues, such as the woody veins. The sowbugs that roll up like armadillos are known as pill bugs.

Figure – 9.6: Sow Bugs

9.13.1.1.10 Pillbugs

Pillbugs look similar to sow bugs and also graze on decaying vegetation but are more flexible. They can roll themselves into a ball to protect themselves, which gives them their common nick-name: "roly-polys."

Organic matter in Soil

Figure – 9.7: Pillbugs

9.13.1.1.11 Mites

Mites are the second most common invertebrate found in compost. They are transparent-bodied creatures with eight leg-like jointed appendages. Some can be seen with the naked eye and others are microscopic. Some scavenge in leaves, rotten wood, fungi, and other organic debris. Others are predators and feed on nematodes, eggs, insect larvae, and other mites and springtails. Considered pests in fermenting industries such as wineries and cheese factories, they are not pests in the compost pile.

9.13.1.1.12 Worms

Worms play an important part in breaking down organic materials and forming finished compost. As red worms process organic materials, they coat their wastes with a mucus film that binds small particles together into stable aggregates and prevents nutrients from leaching out with rainwater. These stable aggregates give the soil a loose and well-draining structure. Earth-worms pull organic materials into the mineral soil along many burrows. As a result of the worm's well-deserved reputation for being excellent decomposers, many people think that it's a great idea to add extra worms to their compost pile. This is unnecessary. Let the worms find their way into the pile when the conditions are right. They prefer the pile when it is cooler, so adding worms could lead to their quick demise in a hot, steamy pile.

9.13.1.2 Level Two - Secondary Consumers

This level includes both herbivores and carnivores: nematodes, protozoa, rotifers, soil flat-worms, springtails, some types of mites, and feather-winged beetles.

9.13.1.2.1 Nematodes

Nematodes or roundworms, are tiny, cylindrical, and often transparent microscopic worms that are the most abundant invertebrates in the soil. Typically, less than one millimeter in length, a handful of decaying compost can contain several million nematodes. Under a magnifying lens, nematodes resemble fine human hair. They can be classified into three categories:

a) Those that eat decaying vegetation
b) Those that are predators on other nematodes, bacteria, algae, protozoa
c) Those that can be serious pests in gardens where they suck the juices of plant roots, especially root vegetables.

Though, there are pest forms of nematodes, most of those found in soil and compost is beneficial.

9.13.1.2.2 Protozoa

Protozoa are the simplest form of the animal organism. Even though they are single-celled and microscopic, they are larger and have more complex activities than most bacteria. Protozoa obtain their food from organic matter in the same way bacteria do, but because they are present in far fewer numbers than bacteria, they play a much smaller part in the composting process.

9.13.1.2.3 Rotifers

Rotifers are minute worms, which usually have one or two groups of vibrating cilia on the head. Their bodies are round and divisible into three parts: a head, trunk, and tail. Many forms are aquatic and are generally found in films of water. The rotifers in compost are found in water that adheres to plant substances where they feed on microorganisms.

9.13.1.2.4 Flatworms

Flatworms are, for the most part, general scavengers that graze on a wide variety of things, including animal matter. As their name implies, flatworms are flat and usually quite small in their free-living form. Most flatworms are carnivorous and live in films of water within the compost structure.

9.13.1.2.5 Springtails

Springtails along with nematodes and mites, are extremely numerous in compost. They are very small wingless insects and can be distinguished by their ability to jump when disturbed. They run in and around the particles in the compost

and have a small spring-like structure under the belly that catapults them into the air when the spring catch is triggered. They feed mainly on fungi, although they also eat nematodes and small bits of organic debris. They are a major population controlling factor on fungi.

9.13.1.2.6 Feather-winged beetles

Feather – winged beetles are the smallest of all beetles and possibly of all insects. These beetles are distinguished by their feather-like wings. Some are blind and most live under bark in forests and woodland. Not surprisingly they go unnoticed. Most species feed on fungi.

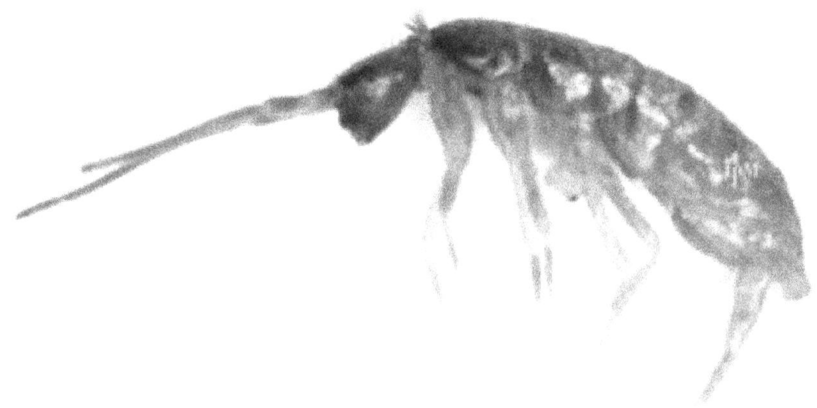

Figure – 9.8: Springtail

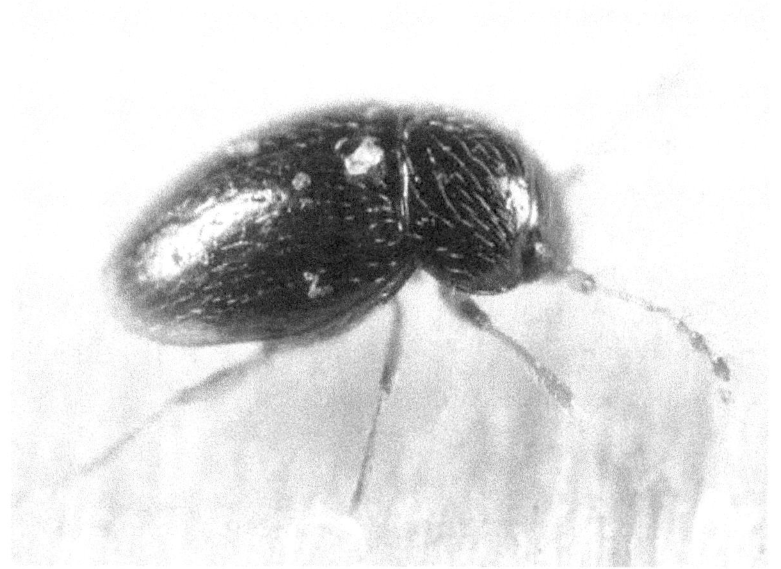

Figure - 9.9: Feather-winged beetles

9.13.1.3 Level Three - Tertiary Consumers

This level is made up of carnivores, or physical decomposers, and includes centipedes, predatory mites, rove beetles, ants, spiders, pseudoscorpions, and earwigs. Most of these creatures function best at medium or mesophilic temperatures, so they will not be in the pile at all times.

9.13.1.3.1 Wolf Spiders

Wolf Spiders are truly wolves of the soil and litter micro-communities. They build no webs, merely run freely hunting their prey, which includes all sizes of arthropods, from mites to centipedes.

9.13.1.3.2 Centipedes

Centipedes are found frequently in soil micro-communities. Centipedes are flattened, segmented worms with 15 or more pairs of legs–one pair per segment. They hatch from eggs laid during the warm months and gradually grow to their adult size. They feed only on living animals, especially insects and spiders.

9.13.1.3.3 Mites

Mites are related to ticks, spiders, and horseshoe crabs because they have six leg-like jointed appendages. Some mites are small enough to be invisible to the naked eye, while some tropical species are up to half an inch in length. Mites reproduce very rapidly, moving through larval, nymph, adult, and dormant stages. They attack plant matter, but some are also second-level consumers, ingesting nematodes, fly larvae, other mites, and springtails.

9.13.1.3.4 Rove Beetles

Rove Beetles are the most common beetles in compost. While feather-winged beetles feed on fungal spores, the larger rove beetles prey on other insects. Beetles are easily visible insects with two pairs of wings, the more forward-placed of these serving as a cover or shield for the folded and thinner back-set ones that are used for flying. These beetles prey on snails, insects, and other small animals. The black rove beetle is an acknowledged predator of snails and slugs. Some people import them to their gardens when slugs become a garden problem.

9.13.1.3.5 Ants

Ants feed on a variety of material, including aphid, honeydew, fungi, seeds, sweets, scraps, other insects, and other ants. Compost provides some of these foods and also provides shelter for nests and hills. Ants will remain only while the pile is relatively cool. Ants prey on first-level consumers and help benefit the composting

process by bringing fungi and other organisms into their nests. The work of ants can make compost richer in phosphorus and potassium by moving minerals from one place to another.

9.13.1.3.6 Pseudoscorpions

Pseudoscorpions are predator s that seize victims with their visible front claws, then inject poison from glands located at the tips of the claws. Pseudoscorpions are so small, their prey includes tiny nematode worms, mites, larvae, and small earthworms.

9.13.1.3.7 Earwigs

Earwigs are large predator's, easily seen with the naked eye. They move about quickly. Some are predators, others feed chiefly on decayed vegetation. *Source: California Integrated Waste Management Board (2005) "Critters in Your Pile;"* http://www.calrecycle.ca.gov/ organics/homecompost/Microbes/Default.htm

9.13.1.4 Unwanted Guests: The pests of the pile

Given a comfortable or nourishing environment, pest species will show up to "get in on the action "Rats are probably the least wanted guests of all. With a hospitable environment and plenty of food, their numbers increase quickly and they may become transmitters of disease. So, it is important to compost food wastes by burying them in the garden, in rodent-proof worm bins, or hot compost piles. Always keep high-protein and fatty food wastes out of the compost pile (meat and fish scraps, bones, cheeses, butter and other dairy products). Many flies, including house flies, can spend their larval phase as maggots in decomposing food wastes. Though they play an important part in the breaking down of all types of organic debris, they are unwanted guests around human house-holds. There are several ways to control their numbers: frequently turn compost piles that contain food (larvae die at high temperatures); cover piles with a dry material that has a high carbon content, such as straw or old grass clippings; or avoiding composting food wastes in yard waste piles.

9.13.1.5 Carbon-to-Nitrogen Ratio

"Greens" and "Browns" All living organisms are made up of large amounts of the element carbon (C) combined with smaller amounts of nitrogen (N). The balance of these elements in a material is called the Carbon-to-Nitrogen ratio (C: N). This ratio is an important factor in determining how easily bacteria can decompose organic waste. The microorganisms in compost use carbon for energy and nitrogen for protein synthesis. The proportion of these two elements used by the bacteria averages about 30 parts carbon to 1 part nitrogen. Given a steady diet at this 30:1

ratio, they can work on organic material very quickly. Most materials available for composting do not have this ratio, so to speed-up composting, our job is to balance the numbers. For instance, a mixture containing equal parts of brown tree leaves (40:1 ratio) and grass clippings (20:1 ratio) would have the ideal 30:1 ratio. This will work best on weight, not volume, basis. Mixing materials of different sizes and textures also helps to provide a well-drained and well-aerated compost pile.

The C: N ratios listed in Table – 9.9 are only guidelines; they are not accurate for every material of that type. For instance, brown grass clippings from a poorly kept lawn will have far less nitrogen content than lush green clippings from an abundantly fertilized lawn. Also, the leaves from different types of trees vary in the C: N balance. It helps to think of materials high in nitrogen as "Greens," and woody, carbon-rich material as "Browns."

Table – 9.9: Average Carbon: Nitrogen Ratios for Organic Materials

High Nitrogen Material	C: N
Grass Clippings	19:1
Sewage Sludge (digested)	16:1
Food Wastes	15:1
Cow Manure	20:1
Horse Manure	25:1
High Carbon Material	**C: N**
Leaves and Foliage	40-80:1
Bark	100-130:1
Paper	170:1
Wood and Sawdust	300-700:1

The best way to become familiar with this balancing is to be specific about it at first, then relax into an intuitive assessment of what a pile needs. Some people like to think in terms of half brown and half green material when building a compost pile out of kitchen and yard wastes. While this may not give the optimum C: N balance, it is a useful rule of thumb for those new to composting and not familiar with the materials. It can be thought of as a chef varying the ingredients for a recipe. Be curious, write down the type and quantity of materials used, and take note of the temperature the pile reaches and the quality of the finished compost.

Organic matter in Soil

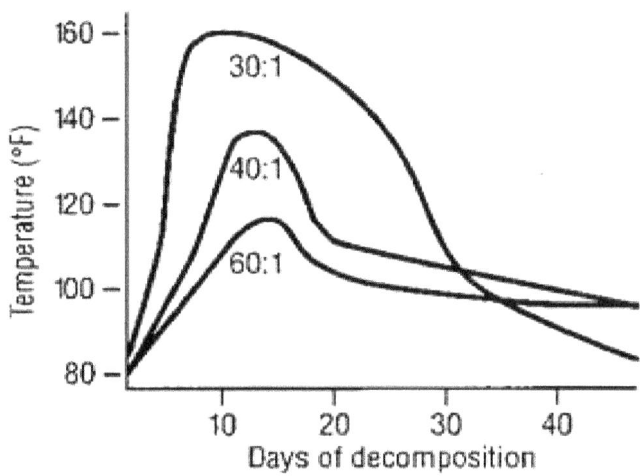

Figure – 9.10: Carbon: Nitrogen ratio effects on composting

9.13.1.6 Surface Area

A melting block of ice is a great analogy for organic materials in the compost. When the block is large it melts quite slowly, but when it is broken into smaller pieces the surface area increases and the melting increases. Similarly, when organic materials are chopped or shredded into smaller pieces, the composting process speeds up. With more surface area exposed, decomposer bacteria have more food easily available so they can reproduce and grow more quickly. It is not essential to break organic materials into small pieces to compost them, it just speeds the process. Sometimes, such as when using Mulches, slow decomposition is advantageous.

9.13.1.7 Moisture and Aeration

All life on earth needs a certain amount of water and air to sustain itself. The compost pile is no different. The amounts of air and water in a compost pile form a delicate balance that must be maintained for rapid decomposition to take place. At less than 40 percent moisture, the bacteria are slowed by the lack of water. At greater than 60 percent moisture, there is not enough air for aerobic decomposition and anaerobic bacteria can take over the pile. Viewed as a microorganism farm, the moisture needs of the pile may need to be tended to just as the farmer tends to the irrigation of crops. Fortunately, there is a simple rule of thumb: compost should be about as moist as a wrung-out sponge. It should be moist to the touch but yield no liquid when squeezed. This level of moisture provides a thin film of water on materials for the decomposer organisms while still al-lowing air into their surroundings. If the pile is too wet, it should be turned (pulled apart and restocked).

Organic matter in Soil

This will allow air back into the pile and loosen up the materials for better draining. A pitchfork is the best tool for turning compost piles. Shovels are not very useful for picking up loose, mixed yard waste. If the pile is too dry, it can be soaked from above with a trickling hose. However, more effective practice is to turn the pile and re-wet the materials in the process. Once dry, certain materials such as dead leaves, sawdust, hay, straw, and some dried weeds and vegetables will shed water or absorb it only on their surface. These dry materials must be gradually wetted until they glisten with moisture. Then they should be mixed until the water has been absorbed into their fibers.

9.13.1.8 Volume

A pile should be large enough to hold heat and small enough to admit air to the center. As a rule of thumb, the *minimum* dimensions of a pile should be 3ft by 3ft to hold heat. The *maximum* dimensions that will allow air to the center of the pile are 5ft by 5ft by any length. There are ways around this rule of thumb. By insulating the sides of the pile, higher temperatures can be maintained in a much smaller volume. Although labor-intensive, it works. By turning a pile or using "ventilation stacks" in the center of the pile, dimensions larger than 5 feet wide are possible. However, a pile this large is unnecessary in most backyard situations.

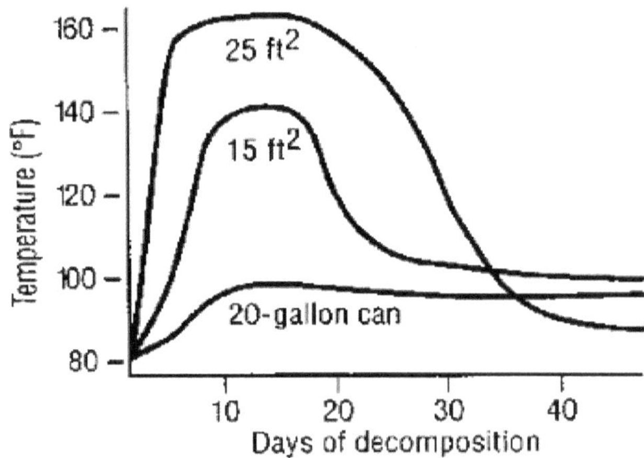

Figure - 9.11: Pile volume effects on composting

9.13.1.9 Time and Temperature

The hotter the pile, the faster the composting process. Temperature is dependent on many factors: carbon to nitrogen ratios, surface area, moisture content, and aeration. Also, remember that only fresh materials will heat up. With proper

consideration of these temperatures, piles can be built and the composting process is quicker. If time is less important, a cooler, slower pile can be built with less attention given to the details of materials used and the environment provided for them. This low-maintenance method of composting will still create an excellent compost.

9.13.1.10 Compost Benefits

Most of the wastes that made up the pile are no longer recognizable in the finished compost, except for some persistent, woody parts. What remains is dark, loose, crumbly material that resembles rich soil. The volume of the finished compost has been reduced by about 30 to 50 percent because of biochemical break-down and water respiration. The compost is now ready to be used for growing new plants and beginning the cycle over again. Compost will improve the quality of almost any soil. The main benefit is to improve the "structure" of the soil. The structure of a soil determines its ability to drain well, store adequate moisture, and meet the many needs of healthy plants. Although compost provides important nutrients, it is not a substitute for fertilizers. More important than the nutrients supplied by compost, is its ability to make existing nutrients more easily available to plants.

9.13.1.10.1 Soil Structure

The value of compost as a soil amendment is suggested by its appearance. Even a casual observation of soil amended with compost shows that it is made up of many round, irregular "aggregates." Aggregates are groups of particles loosely bound together by the secretions of worms and compost bacteria. If these aggregates are rubbed between a finger and thumb, they break down into smaller aggregates. In between and within the aggregates themselves are many small air channels like the empty spaces left in a jar of marbles. A well-structured soil with lots of small aggregates stays loose and easy to cultivate. The channels that aggregates create through the soil allow plant roots and moisture to penetrate easily. The smaller pores within the aggregates loosely hold moisture until a plant needs it. The larger pore spaces between the aggregates allow excess water to drain out and air to circulate and warm the soil. By encouraging the formation of aggregates, compost improves the structure of every type of soil: silt, sand, or clay. In loose sandy soils, compost helps to bind unconsolidated particles together to retain water and nutrients that would normally wash right through. Added to a clay or silt soil, compost breaks up the small tightly bound particles and forms larger aggregations, which allow water to drain and air to penetrate.

Organic matter in Soil

9.13.1.10.2 Nutrient Content

Dark, loose compost looks like it should be rich in nutrients. Indeed, compost contains a variety of the basic nutrients that plants require for healthy growth. Of special importance are the micro-nutrients present in compost, such as iron, manganese, copper, and zinc. They are only needed in small doses, like vitamins in our diet, but without them, plants have difficulty extracting nutrients from other foods. Micro-nutrients are often absent from commercial fertilizers, so compost is an essential dietary supplement in any soil. Compost also contains small amounts of the macro-nutrients that plants need in larger doses. Macro-nutrients include nitrogen, phosphorous, potassium, calcium, and magnesium. These nutrients are usually applied in measured amounts through commercial fertilizers and lime. The three numbers listed on fertilizer bags (e.g., 10- 10-10) refer to the percentage of the three primary macro-nutrients available in the fertilizer-- nitrogen, phosphorous, and potassium (N-P-K). Although compost generally contains small amounts of these macro-nutrients, they are typically present in forms that are not readily available to plants. When applied in 4- to 6-inch layers, compost may provide significant amounts of these nutrients. However, due to the variability and slow release of major nutrients, compost is considered a supplement to fertilization with more reliable nutrient sources.

9.13.1.10.3 Nutrient Storage and Availability

Understanding how compost can store nutrients and make them available when needed by plants requires a closer look. When viewing compost through a microscope that enlarges things 1,000 times, individual compost particles resemble aggregates that are not observed with the unaided eye. Like the aggregates, individual particles of compost contain many porous channels. Just as the channels in the aggregates provide space to store water, these spaces in compost particles provide spaces to store nutrients. The sides of the channels provide vast surfaces inside the particles where individual ions of minerals and fertilizers can cling. These ions are given up to plant roots as the plants require them. Thus, compost can store nutrients that might otherwise wash through a sandy soil or be locked up in spaces of clay soil. The ions clinging to the surfaces of our compost particles tend to be those that give the soil a "neutral" pH. A measure of soil acidity or alkalinity is its pH. The acidity or alkalinity of soil affects the availability of nutrients to plants. Most important plant nutrients are relatively easily available to plants at a pH range of 5.5 to 7.5. At pH levels above this range (alkaline) or below this range (acid), essential nutrients become chemically bound in the soil and are unavailable to plants. Yard debris compost typically has a pH range of 5.5 to 7.5. When mixed into soil, this compost will help keep the pH at optimum levels for nutrient availability.

Organic matter in Soil

9.13.1.10.4 Beneficial Soil Life

Taking a step back from the microscopic view, another beneficial characteristic of compost is evident. The presence of red worms, centipedes, sowbugs, and others shows that compost is a healthy living material. The presence of decomposer organisms means that there is still some organic material being slowly broken down and releasing nutrients. They are also indicators of balanced soil ecology, which includes organisms that keep diseases and pests in check. Many experiments have shown that the rich soil life in compost helps to control diseases and pests that might otherwise overrun a more sterile soil lacking natural checks against their spread.

Particle Size Effects on Composting

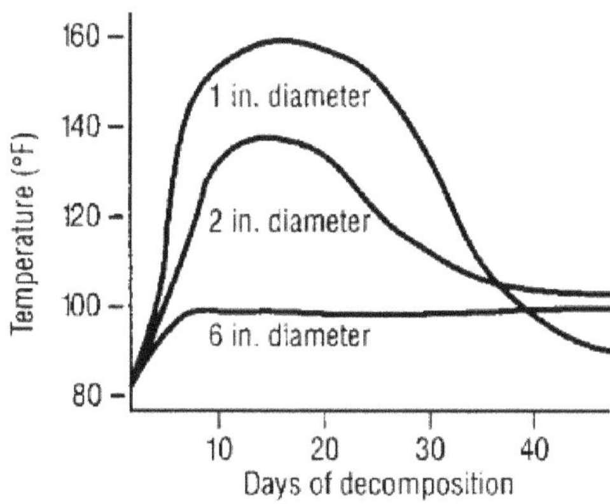

Figure – 9.12: Particle size effects on composting

Turning Frequency Effects on Composting

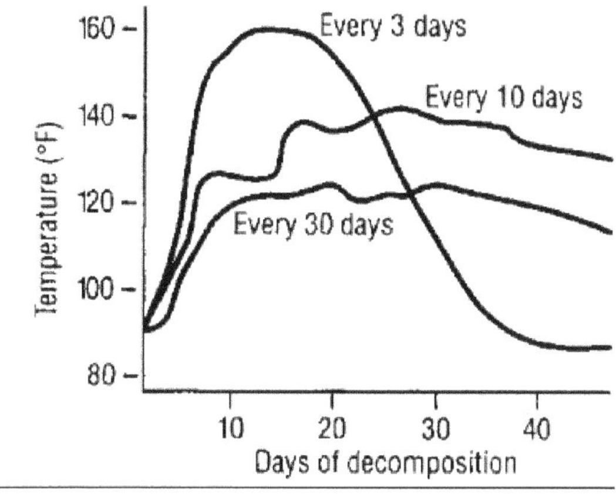

Figure – 9.13: Turning frequency effects on composting

10
HARVESTING THE COMPOST AND WORMS

There are three basic ways to separate the worms from the finished compost. One way involves moving the finished compost. One way involves moving the finished compost and worms over to one side of the bin and adding new bedding material and food waste to the other side. Worms in the finished compost move over to the few bedding with the fresh food waste. The finished compost can then be removed.

10.1. Methods of Harvesting Worms

10.1.1 General Method

Worm harvesting is usually carried out to sell the worms (see Section 6.2.2), rather than to start new worm beds. Expanding the operation (new beds) can be accomplished by splitting the beds, that is, removing a portion of the bed to start a new one and replacing the material with new bedding and feed. When worms are sold, however, they are usually separated, weighed, and then transported in a relatively sterile medium, such as peat moss. To accomplish this, the worms must first be separated from the bedding and vermicompost. There are three basic categories of methods used by growers to harvest worms: manual, migration, and mechanical (Bogdanov, 1996).

10.1.2 Manual Methods

Manual methods are the ones used by hobbyists and smaller-scale growers, particularly those who sell worms to the home-vermicomposting or bait market. In essence, manual harvesting involves hand-sorting or picking the worms directly from the compost by hand. This process can be facilitated by taking advantage of the fact that worms avoid light. If the material containing worms is dumped in a pile on a flat surface with a light above, the worms will quickly dive below the surface. The harvester can then remove a layer of compost, stopping when worms become visible

Harvesting the Compost and Worms

again. This process is repeated several times until there is nothing left on the table except a huddled mass of worms under a thin covering of compost. These worms can then be quickly scooped into a container, weighed, and prepared for delivery. There are several minor variations and/or enhancements on this method, such as using a container instead of a flat surface, or making several piles at once, so that the person harvesting can move from one to another, returning to the first one in time to remove the next layer of compost. They are all labor-intensive, however, and only make sense if the operation is small and the value of the worms is high.

10.1.3 Self-Harvesting (Migration) Methods

These methods, like some of the methods used in vermicomposting, are based on the worms tend to migrate to new regions, either to find new food or to avoid undesirable conditions, such as dryness or light. Unlike the manual methods described above, however, they often make use of simple mechanisms, such as screens or onion bags. The screening method is very common and easy to use. A box is constructed with a screen bottom. The mesh is usually ¼", although 1/8" can be used as well. There are two different approaches. The downward-migration system is similar to the manual system, in that the worms are forced downward by strong light. The difference with the screen system is that the worms go down through the screen into a prepared, pre-weighed container of moist peat moss. Once the worms have all gone through, the compost in the box is removed and a new batch of worm-rich compost is put in. The process is repeated until the box with the peat moss has reached the desired weight. Like the manual method, this system can be set up in several locations at once, so that the worm harvester can move from one box to the next, with no time wasted waiting for the worms to migrate. The upward-migration system is similar, except that the box with the mesh bottom is placed directly on the warm bed. It has been filled with a few centimeters of damp peat moss and then sprinkled with a food attractive to worms, such as chicken mash, coffee grounds, or fresh cattle manure. The box is removed and weighed after visual inspection indicates that sufficient worms have moved up into the material. This system is used extensively in Cuba, with the difference that large onion bags are used instead of boxes. The advantage of this system is that the worm beds are not disturbed. The main disadvantage is that the harvested worms are in the material that contains a fair amount of unprocessed food, making the materials and opening up the possibility of heating inside the package if the worms are shipped. The latter problem can be avoided by removing any obvious food and allowing a bit of time for the worms to consume what is left before packaging.

Harvesting the Compost and Worms

10.1.4 Mechanical Methods

Mechanical harvesters are the quickest and easiest method for separating worms from vermicompost. The following description is from **Bogdanov (1996).** The mechanical harveste is a trommel device, a rotating cylinder about 8-10 feet in length and 2-3 feet in diameter. The cylinder walls are composed of screen material of different mesh sizes. The cylinder is rotated by a small electric motor mounted on one end of the cylinder. The trommel is set a an angle; at the upper end of the rotating trommel worms and their bedding including castings are added. As the cylinder rotates, the castings fall through the screen. The worms 'ride' the entire distance of the trommel and pass through the lower end into a wheelbarrow."

10.2 Components of a Commercial Unit

Commercial units have to be developed based on the availability of cow dung locally. If some big dairy is functioning then such a unit will be an associated activity. Commercial units must not be designed based on imported cow dung. The philosophy is *in-situ* development using "Natural Resources".

10.2.1 Sheds

For a vermicomposting unit, whether small or big, this is an essential item and is required for securing the vermi beds. They could be of a thatched roof supported by bamboo rafters and purlins, wooden or steel trusses and stone/ RCC pillars. Locally available roofing materials or HDPE sheets may also be used in roofing to keep the capital investment at a reasonably lower level. If the size is so chosen as to prevent the wetting of beds due to rain on a windy day, they could be open sheds. While designing the sheds adequate room/pathways have to be left around the beds for easy movement of the laborers attending to the filling and harvesting the beds.

10.2.2 Vermi-beds

Normally the beds have 0.3 to 0.6 m height depending on the provision for drainage of excess water. Care should be taken to make the bed with uniform height over the entire width to avoid low production owing to low bed volumes. The bed width should not be more than 1.5 m to allow easy access to the center of the bed.

10.2.3 Land

About 0.5-0.6 acres of land will be needed to set up a vermiculture production. The center will have at least 6-8 sheds for convenience and a dedicated area for finished products. It should also have a bore well and pump set or watering

Harvesting the Compost and Worms

arrangement and other equipment as described in the scheme economics. The land can be taken on lease for at least 10-15 years.

10.2.4 Buildings

When the activity is taken up on a large scale on commercial lines, a considerable amount may have to be spent on buildings to house the office, store the raw material and finished product, provide minimum accommodation to the Manager and workers. The cost of the buildings along with the electrification of these buildings and the vermi-sheds may be included under this item.

10.2.5 Seed Stock

This is an important item requiring considerable expenditure. Though the worms multiply fast to give the required numbers over 6 months to a year, it may not be wise to wait till such a time having invested in the infrastructure heavily. Thus, worms @ 1 kg per m^3 of bed volume should be adequate to start with and to build up the required population in about two or three cycles without unduly affecting the estimated production.

10.2.6 Fencing and Roads/Paths

The site area needs development for the construction of structures and development of roads and pathways for easy movement of hand-drawn trolleys/wheelbarrows for conveying the raw material and the finished products to and from the vermi-sheds. The entire area has to be fenced to prevent trespass by animals and other unwanted elements. These could be estimated based on the length of the 4 peripheries of the farm and the length and type of roads/paths required. The costs on fencing and formation of roads should be kept low as these investments are essential for a production unit, yet would not lead to an increase in production.

10.2.7 Water Supply System

As the beds have to be kept moist always with about 50% moisture content, there is a need to plan for a water source, lifting mechanism, and a system of conveying and applying the water to the vermi-beds. Drippers with round the clock flow arrangement would be quite handy for continuous supply and saving on water. Such a water supply system requires a considerable initial investment. However, it reduces the operational cost of hand watering sand proves economical in the long run. The cost of these items would depend on the capacity of the unit and the type of water supply chosen.

10.2.8 Machinery

Farm machinery and implements are required for cutting (shredding) the raw material into small pieces, conveying shredded raw material to the vermi-sheds, loading, unloading, collection of compost, loosening of beds for aeration, shifting of the compost before packing and for air drying of the compost, automatic packing and stitching for the efficient running of the unit.

10.2.9 Transportation

For any vermicomposting unit, the transport arrangement is a must. When the source of raw material is away from the production unit, off-site transport becomes a major item of investment. A large-sized unit with about 1000 tonnes per annum capacity may require three tones capacity mini- truck. With small units particularly with the availability of raw material near the site, expending on transport facilities may become infructuous. On –site transport facilities like manually drawn trolleys to convey raw materisl and finished products between the storage point and vermicompost sheds.

10.2.10 Furniture

A reasonable amount could also be considered for furnishing the office-cum-stores including the storage racks and other office types of equipment. This will enhance the efficiency of operations.

11
CONSTRUCTION OF WORM BIN

Bins can be made of wood or plastic, or from recycled containers like old bath tubs, barrels, or trunks. They also can be located inside or outside, depending on your preferences and circumstances. As red wigglers tend to be surface feeders, bins should be no more than 8 to 12 inches deep. Bedding and food wastes tend to pack down in deeper bins, forcing air out. Resulting anaerobic conditions can cause foul odors and death of the worms. The length and width of the bin will depend on whether it is to be stationary or portable. It also depends on the amount of food waste your family produces each week. A good rule of thumb is to provide one square foot of surface area per pound of waste in your bin. Wooden bins have the advantage that they are more absorbent and provide better insulation. Do not use redwood or other highly aromatic woods that may kill the worms. Plastic tends to keep the compost too moist. Plastic, however, tends to be less messy and easier to maintain. Be sure containers are well cleaned and have never stored pesticides or other chemicals. Drilling air/drainage holes (Â¼- to Â½-inch diameter) in the bottom and sides of the bin will ensure good water drainage and air circulation. Place the bin on bricks or wooden blocks in a tray to catch excess water that drains from the bin. The resulting compost tea can be used as a liquid fertilizer around the home landscape. Each bin should have a cover to conserve moisture and exclude light. Worms prefer darkness. Bins can be covered with straw mulch or moist burlap to ensure darkness while providing good air ventilation. Outside bins may require a lid to exclude scavengers and other unwanted pests. Outdoor bins should be insulated from the cold to protect the worms. One option is to dig a rectangular hole 12 inches deep and line the sides with wooden planks. The bottomless box can then be filled with hole 12 inches deep and line the sides with wooden planks. The bottomless box can then be filled with appropriate bedding material, food wastes, and worms. Food wastes can be continually added as they accumulate. The pile should be kept damp and dark for optimum worm activity. During the winter, soil

can be piled against the edges of the bin and straw placed on top to protect the worms from cold weather. Do not add food waste to outdoor bins the winter because this could expose the worms to freezing weather.

11.1 How to Feed Earthworm

The earthworm will need a little help from you in the preparation of some of the materials. When feeding the scraps if at all possible chop or break them into small pieces as it will be easier for the worms to process. Leave the scraps in a container for a few days so bacteria will start forming because worms love bacteria. Be sure the overall mix, (or any individual waste), is moist, about like a blueberry muffin or sponge cake. In the case of vermicomposting of kitchen waste, most food wastes can be put directly on the warm bed just as it comes from the table. Just scatter it around the top of the bed.

11.2 Feeds and bedding

Some materials can serve as feed and bedding. Successful producers provide for their livestock's (worms) need for both. Both the feed and the bedding will be consumed by the diverse population of organisms in a worm production system and both will need to be replaced as the material is converted to worm castings.

11.3 Worm Bin Composting

Combine shredded paper, soil and just enough water to dampen everything. Put the mixture into the tall bin and fill the bin about three inches deep. Add your Worms to the mixture and let them get used to it for a day before feeding them. Make sure the mixture is very moist, but not forming puddles of water.

11.4 Feed

Worms eat a wide variety of organic materials or, more accurately, a wide variety of the microbes that feed on organic materials. Almost any plant or animal waste could be used as worm feed. But remember that, like other livestock, worms need vitamins, minerals, protein and carbohydrates. Feeds should contain more carbohydrates and cellulose than protein. Usually, the feed has nitrogen and is balanced by the high level of carbon in the bedding. A carbon-to-nitrogen ratio of 30 parts carbon to 1 part nitrogen is about right for a worm production system. Too much nitrogen creates ammonia, which is toxic to worms and to many of the microbes that the production system relies on. Excess carbon slows microbial activity and reduces overall productivity. Fat or oily materials such as soybean or sunflower meals should be avoided because oil slows bacterial breakdown, shifting the pH toward an acid bed. Animal by-products, dairy products and meat are generally

avoided because they attract flies, rodents and other pests. However, animal waste – especially livestock manure mixed with straw or sawdust – is good for a worm business because the feed and bedding are already combined. Use good sanitary procedures when handling raw manure to prevent the spread of infection from possible pathogens in the manure. Worms have no teeth, so it is best to use small feed particles. If you grind feed materials very finely, worms can utilize them more readily, but be sure that there are enough coarse materials for bedding so that the materials will not pack tightly and limit oxygen. Another way to reduce particle size is to soak feed before adding it to the bed. Worms have gizzards, as chickens do, and need some kind of grit to help them reduce the size of the food particles they eat. Adding sand or clean garden soil periodically will help the worms consume their feed. If the bed is tending toward a pH that is too acidic, a small amount of agricultural lime (calcium carbonate) can serve as the grit and neutralize the living conditions. A limited number of egg shells will also serve this purpose, but watch for pest problems. Bacteria, fungi and other soil-dwelling microbes also help break organic material into usable particle sizes. Bacteria and molds begin to digest organic matter very quickly. Their activity softens and breaks down food to further prepare it for the worms. Scientists believe that microbes themselves constitute a sizable portion of the worm diet. Protozoa may in fact be the dominant nutrient source. However, rotifers, nematodes, bacteria and fungi – as well as the decomposing remains of plants and other animals – are also eaten and probably provide some animal manures (no antibiotics or deworming medications) cardboard, shredded hay, either legume or grass types waste products and paper products sewage sludge food scraps (avoid meat and dairy) synthetic feeds almost any decaying organic material.

11.5 Do not feed

Meat scraps or bones, fish, greasy or oily foods, fat, tobacco or pet or human manure.

Figure – 11.1: Worms with vegetable scraps and paper bedding

This is why worms like feed materials that have already started to spoil. Monitor how quickly the feed is being processed, and don't overfeed. Producers who top-feed either remove unused feed or to wait until visible feed has been consumed before adding more. You might choose to offer a fattening ration just before harvest if your system goal is to raise worms to sell to the bait market or if you are selling some worms as breeding stock. Because maximum growth is desired, you might purchase feed formulated for this purpose. If you would rather formulate your own ration, a commonly used recipe contains the following ingredients, very finely ground:

- 5 parts chicken starter (high-protein corn, ground)
- 2 parts bran (wheat or rice)
- 1 part wheat flour
- 1 part powdered milk
- 1 part agricultural lime
- 3 parts ground alfalfa.

If the focus of your operation is to use worms to process plant or animal wastes into vermicompost, few purchased inputs are required. Look around your area for confined livestock operations, canning factories and mushroom facilities for potential sources of waste. Groceries and restaurants are other possibilities if vegetable matter can be separated from animal and other waste products. Pre-consumer wastes are easier to handle than postconsumer garbage. Since landfills in many areas will not accept organic materials, some establishments might pay you to receive their wastes. This tipping fee is commonly charged for the disposal of garbage. Similarly, livestock manure is subjected to legal restrictions so that it doesn't contaminate nearby water sources. Diverting these waste streams to worm production is an opportunity for the entrepreneurial worm farmer.

11.6 Manure for feed or bedding

Manure is a great feed or bedding material. Try to find a trustworthy source of manure that is free of antibiotics, dewormers and other chemical medications. Check for an acceptable level of urine and salts. If the product is consistent, and you are observant about your system, you will not need to test it often. A pile of fresh manure, even when mixed with straw or sawdust bedding, immediately begins a thermophilic (heat-producing) composting process. Bacteria cause this activity and the resulting compost is microbe-rich, but make sure the thermal composting process is done before using this manure in your worm beds. Many vermicompost systems rely on thermal composting prior to feeding the organic material to the worms. Pre-

composting, as it is sometimes called, can disable viable seeds and kill some human pathogens that may have been in the feedstock. Pre-composting takes much less time than completely composting the feedstock material. Since pre-composting is designed to allow some of the potential heat to dissipate, it is usually a short (often two weeks) but closely monitored process. Materials are combined and the pile is built. Proper moisture and aeration help create an active pile that heats to 160 degrees F for three days. The compost is often turned and allowed to heat a second time. After this stage, the material can be cooled and carefully added to a working bin.

11.7 Bedding material

Bedding for bins can be made from shredded newspapers (non-glossy), computer paper, or cardboard; shredded leaves, straw, hay, or dead plants; sawdust; peat moss; or compost or aged (or composted) manure. Peat moss should be soaked for 24 hours in the water, then lightly wrung out to ensure it is sufficiently moist. Grass clippings should be allowed to age before use because they may decompose too quickly, causing the compost to heat up. Bedding materials high in cellulose are best because they help aerate the bin so the worms can breathe. Varying the bedding material provides a richer source of nutrients. Some soil or sand can be added to help provide grit for the worm digestive systems. Allow the bedding material to set for several days to make sure it doesn't heat up (and allow it to cool before adding worms). The bedding material should be thoroughly moistened (about the consistency of a damp sponge) before adding the worms. Fill the bin three-quarters full of moist bedding, lifting it gently afterward to create air space for the worms to breathe and to control odors.

11.8 Testing material for use as bedding

Fill a small container that has aeration holes with the prospective bedding material. Introduce a small number of worms into the container. If the worms are still there 12 hours later, it is safe to use the material as bedding. If they are dead or have crawled out of the container, further processing is needed. Leach or age the manure for a longer period and test again before using it as bedding. Example - worms will process the bedding as well as the feed, so why make the distinction? Bedding is typically a carbonaceous material that will break down more slowly than the feed. It is usually a coarse material that won't pack tightly and therefore maintains air pockets within the growth chamber. It helps to absorb excess moisture from feedstock as well. Some commercial systems use peat moss as bedding, but this is an expensive, nonrenewable input that might be better used in other applications. Coconut coir, a renewable resource, has replaced peat moss in many systems. Its disadvantage, from a sustainability perspective, is that it is transported long

distances. Sustainable, economic opportunity in worm production lies in using easily obtainable inexpensive or free materials for as many of the inputs as possible.

11.9 Possible bedding materials

Shredded paper (newsprint, paper bags, cardboard, office paper, but not cross-cut shredded) sawdust (but not from redwoods, pine or other aromatic softwoods; test first) Composted animal manure (cow, horse, rabbit) shredded, decaying leaves, straw peat moss (consider sustainability and cost issues) coconut coir (consider transportation cost and sustainability).

11.10 Worm bin ecology

A successful worm bin is an ecosystem containing a wide diversity of plants (fungi, bacteria, and molds) and animals, all adapted to similar conditions. There are many more species than just the worm that the system is managed for. These critters, both microscopic and visible, are interdependent; they all work toward breaking down and stabilizing the organic materials in a worm bin. Because worms don't have teeth and have only rudimentary digestive fluids, they depend on other creatures for help to make nutrients available. The large, visible organisms reduce the size of particles in the bed so that the smaller creatures have access to more surface area. Microorganisms use their enzymes or digestive acids to process food for themselves, which makes the organic material more available to worms and other critters in the system. Each species has a niche. Any given organism feeds on materials or other organisms in the bed and is likely to become food to others in the ecosystem. To the new producer, some of the organisms in the worm ecosystem will be unfamiliar and might cause concern. However, most are not dangerous to the worms and are extremely beneficial to the efficient functioning of the system. Few of them eat living plant material, so they are rarely a danger to plants that will receive the vermicompost. These descriptions are very brief, serving as an introduction to the residents of the worm-producing ecosystem that you are managing. Learn more about each of them as you observe them in the system. If certain critters seem to be overwhelming the system, study them, learn what conditions are causing the increase and adjust your management to bring the system back into equilibrium. animals that might threaten worms in a production system as well as benign critters that are potential competitors for feed. Because this is an extremely intricate biological system, using chemicals to control any member within it will affect the others. If you use chemicals, they may persist in the bedding or castings. Later, when the material is added to the soil, it might be hazardous to the growing plants.

Construction of Worm Bin

11.10.1 Diseases

Worms are not generally susceptible to diseases; however, they are sensitive to conditions in their environment. Protein poisoning or sour crop will result from the accumulation of unused feed in the bin. When this happens, the bed becomes acidic and gases are released into the bedding.

Symptoms include

Swollen or burst clitellum Knots along with the worm's body worms that are stringy or crawl around aimlessly on the bed's surface worms that stay low in the beds and refuse to come up to eat worms that turn white and die in the bedding. An increase in the population of acid-loving worm bin residents.

11.10.2 Separating worms from vermicompost

No matter what product you're selling, separating worms from vermicompost is necessary. If you're selling the worms, the larger worms may be separated by one of the methods below and then fed a fattening feed ration to increase their size or to clear their guts if they are being sold as feed. You should periodically harvest to redistribute worms, even if they are not being sold, to keep populations from becoming overcrowded. Start with a 30-day harvest interval (after your production area is fully occupied) and adjust it according to your system's requirements. Sorting systems use worms' natural aversion to light, their tendency to move upward to fresh food offered, and mechanical screening devices to separate worms from the vermicompost.

11.10.2.1 Hand sorting worms

Removing the top 3-4 inches of bedding from the growing area to a sorting table is a labor-intensive way to sort worms. A strong light is maintained in the work area so that as layers of vermicompost are brushed away the worms are exposed and immediately burrow into the remaining material. The larger worms move down faster than smaller ones so that the top layer of bedding and the smaller worms are swept back into the growing area. The worms are allowed to move to the bottom again. After several sweepings, the remaining bedding is swept toward the center of the table and the worms are allowed to move to the bottom and the top of this pile is swept away. Finally, the large worms are hand-picked into containers with damp bedding and ready for further fattening or immediate sale.

11.10.2.2 Using screens to separate worms

The simplest method of screening worms from their bedding involves shaking a box with a screen bottom. The screen size allows vermicompost to fall through and the worms remain in the box. When screens of different sizes are used, the Vermicompost can be separated from the small worms and eggs as well. This method has obvious drawbacks because of size limitations and labor requirements. Some production systems are based on using stacked boxes with screen bottoms. As the feed and bedding are used in a box, another box with fresh feed and bedding is placed on top of it. Worms naturally migrate away from the castings-rich environment to the next level above it. At intervals, another similar box with fresh bedding and feed is added to the top of the stack. After the worms have moved up, the bottom box is removed and the vermicompost is processed for sale. Another harvest method uses a screen wire that is placed in the bed. Again, fresh food and bedding are placed on the screen wire to entice the worms away from the worked material toward the bottom of the bed. The worms move up through the screening and feed near the surface. After the worms have been feeding and growing above the screen for some time, the screen is removed with the worms in it. What remains below the screen is mostly vermicompost ready to be processed for use or sale. The worms' natural inclination to move upward and toward fresh bedding is used to harvest worms in windrow systems as well. This is the most common way to prepare the finished vermicompost for harvest. New bedding is placed on the top of the window and worms move into it. When most of the worms have moved, the top layer of the window is removed to start the next one, leaving the castings behind. Some systems place the new bedding next to the existing window, forming a wedge, but the separation of worms from vermicompost is less complete.

11.10.2.3 Handling the worms

Whatever method is chosen to separate worms from vermicompost, consider the worms' needs during the process. The worms will die if exposed to light or very dry conditions for too long. Wear damp gloves to handle the worms and move the worms that will stay in your system to fresh bedding as soon as possible. Worms that will be shipped should be quickly weighed and placed into the damp medium they will be shipped in.

11.10.3 Marketing worms and vermicompost

Marketing your product is an area to address long before you have anything to sell. It doesn't matter if you will be selling worms or vermicompost, you must have a buyer if you are going to make money. Where will you sell your product? Will you sell wholesale or retail? Who are your customers in each case? Approach

and begin to educate potential buyers as you develop the rest of the business. As your market grows, you can increase production as well. The worm market, though stable, is not growing much. The vermicompost market is more likely to grow because of these trends: Increased interest and understanding about recycling. Awareness about sustainable systems Laws banning organic materials from landfills Expansion of the market for organic farming products Increased awareness in the general public about vermicomposting (Quillian, 1998).

11.10.3.1 *Selling worms*

The main markets for worms are:

- As bait
- For feed
- For household food waste processing

Approach local bait stores and ask if they would be interested in buying directly from a local grower rather than a distant seller. When you are in production, provide samples for their consideration. Once you've made a sale, you must provide continuing good service and produce a quality product to cultivate a customer that will buy from you repeatedly. Vending machines that dispense bait are a relatively new development. An excellent location and conscientious servicing can make this option worthwhile. Besides face-to-face sales, the Internet provides another direct sales channel. Create a website that details your products and services. Because most of your customers will be remote, your presentation will compete with all other worm outlets on the internet. Learn the strategies for increasing your website's exposure. You will also have to decide how you will ship your product and set up a secure payment system. Pet stores buy worms as feed for some of their animals. They will probably want to buy live worms. Likewise, pet owners are potential customers. Alternatively, worms can be dried and made into a meal to be used as feed. This worm meal is easier to transport and store than live worms. Producing a meal requires further processing. Can you get a price that justifies the extra expense? Packaging and labeling must also, be considered. Although selling worms to businesses and municipalities that are beginning to process their organic wastes by vermicomposting is a possibility, this is not a large or recurring market. A 2003 scam claimed to be supplying worms for start-up municipal vermicomposting operations. Even if this had been true, it is unlikely that a huge supply of worms would have been required. Each new facility would most likely make one the initial purchase of worms and then maintain a working population without the need for further purchases. Selling to individuals and families who want to use worms to process their waste is another opportunity. However, this is usually a one-time, relatively

small scale. You will need many customers of this type to generate significant worm sales.

11.10.3.2 *Packaging and shipping worms*

Depending on where you will be selling your worms, you will need individual containers or bulk containers for packaging and shipping. If your market is local bait shops, you will probably count or weigh and cup the worms yourself. You or an employee will deliver and provide service to your customers. However, if your market is farther away, packaging and shipping require a different type of system. Ship worms as quickly as possible after harvest and are sure to maintain optimal conditions for their survival. Peter Bogdanov, in his excellent book *Commercial Vermiculture: How to Build a Thriving Business in Redworms,* recommends sphagnum peat moss as a shipping medium. The bedding should be damp and air must be available. Bogdanov has determined that, for his operation, waxed cardboard containers are best for a small to medium amount of worms. Other authors have described many types of containers, including plastic foam, wax-coated paper, and rigid plastic. Breathable paper or cloth bags are also used for bulk shipping. Choose a shipping company according to accessibility and services offered. Since worms will not survive extreme temperatures, plan for their protection. Label the container so people handling them in transit can safeguard the contents. *Live earthworms* and *Perishable* and *Do not expose to extreme temperatures* are suggested. Precooling the shipping medium and worms to 68-72 degrees F results in lower fatalities in hot weather, according to Roy and Dianne Fewell in *As the Worm Turns* (Fewell and Fewell, 2007). Bogdanov recommends doing practice runs by shipping to friends or relatives to make sure your containers, shipping material, and methods will succeed in delivering the worms in good condition. Your first customers will appreciate the results, and you may save the expense of having to repeat orders because you had not perfected your shipping system.

11.10.3.3 *Selling castings or vermicompost*

Vermicompost is a high-quality soil amendment that has been shown to offer growth and yield advantages as well as resistance to plant pests and diseases. Likewise, vermicompost tea has been recognized as a provider of considerable benefits in plant production systems when it is used as a soil drench or a foliar spray. However, the general public and even many businesses that would clearly benefit from its use are often unaware of the advantages of using vermicompost. Do not assume that if you have it, people will buy it.

Plan to educate your customers and develop a market as you generate the product. Spending time and resources with nurseries, landscapers, and garden supply store managers could be well worth your time. Other potential buyers of bulk vermicompost might include organic farmers or turf farms, as well as a golf course and sports field managers. You may even want to conduct trials comparing your product with whatever is currently being used. Perhaps you can help clients set up a trial at their place of business. Remember, once you secure the business of a customer that requires large volumes of materials repeatedly and you can deliver a consistent product, you will be on your way. Some buyers will want to buy small amounts for gardens and others will buy by the truckload. These are issues you must evaluate during your market research. You will need to decide how to sell your product. Who is your target market Will you need to package or The effects of vermicompost and vermicompost teas in plant production systems are being studied at several universities. Although Vermicompost doesn't test high in nitrogen, phosphorus, or potassium, it does contain significant micronutrients. Biological activity is very high, and evidence of plant growth hormones has accumulated. Disease suppression, pest resistance, better growth, and higher yields have been documented and are under investigation. For more information about the research into these qualities – especially if you need it for promoting your product further process the product? If you package the vermicompost, you will likely have to create a legal label; this can be a challenge in itself. Consult with your state Department of Agriculture for applicable regulations. Remember that your vermicompost product must be consistently available and be of dependable quality. These attributes are key to return business

11.10.4 *How to ensure consistent quality vermicompost*

The nutrient content of vermicompost is extremely variable. Although you will see analyses for various manures or vermicomposts, the actual content depends on two main factors:

- The feedstock and bedding
- The environmental conditions under which it is produced

Feedstock and Bedding are the two major inputs. The nutrient analysis of the Vermicompost will reflect these materials. Cattle manure with straw produces a different product from chicken litter with wood shavings. The relative amount of nitrogen and carbon will also affect the composition of the biological community inhabiting the final product (Slocum, 2000).

Construction of Worm Bin

In addition to the nutrient content, the material fed or used as bedding can potentially contain substances toxic to plants or humans. If landscape waste materials are included, be sure they don't contain persistent pesticide residues. Livestock waste can contain residues from medications or feed additives. Know your inputs. Seeds in the feedstock provide an additional challenge. Be sure that no viable seeds make it through the worms or your product might cause weed problems for customers. Such a mistake is not easily fixed, especially when you have lost your customers' trust. Pre-composting the feedstock and bedding materials, if they contain seeds, can prevent such problems. Be very careful with any input that might contain human pathogens that might survive worm processing. Develop a system to handle such resources by isolating them from contact with the finished product, maintaining aerobic production conditions, and separately pre-composting them in a thermal system to ensure that they are safe to use. This is serious business and your liability here is absolute.

The second factor that affects the final product is the environmental conditions in the worm bins. Temperature, moisture, and pH all determine which organisms thrive and which do not. If these conditions are kept constant, the microorganism community will also remain relatively steady. Similarly, the microbes that live in the worm gut processing the organic matter adapt to whatever conditions they are subjected to. Continually changing these conditions reduces the efficiency of your production system and affects the uniformity of the final merchandise (Slocum, 2000). The length of time the material is in the bed affects the final product. If the temperature is not optimal or other environmental conditions are not ideal, worms will take longer to process the same materials. If conditions are not stable, monitor them, and adjust your procedures to ensure the reliability of your product. Your product will be consistent if your production system uses known materials in unvarying proportions. Monitor environmental conditions and establish routines so that you do not have to test often to be confident that your product doesn't vary in content or quality. Check with your local Cooperative Extension Service about testing the macronutrients and content of your product. Many states provide this service. Labs that specialize in testing the biological components of compost or vermicompost are a little harder to find. Consult ATTRA's *Alternative Soil Testing Laboratories* for a list. When you bag your product to sell, the label will probably be regulated by law. Check with your state Department of Agriculture for information on what is required.

Construction of Worm Bin

11.10.5 Reasons that current demand for vermicompost is low

- Lack of consistent supply
- Lack of large producers
- Uneducated consumers
- Lack of tests for content and quality
- Lack of field-tested research
- Lack of research in commercial settings (Quillian, 1998)

11.10.6 Steps toward developing a national vermicompost market

- Ideally, some of these would be accomplished by a producers' association
- Consolidate existing research results and knowledge into a useful form.
- Field test vermicompost in a commercial setting. Producers must:
- Work with growers' associations and university agriculture departments to fund and/or conduct field research
- Work with Sustainable Agriculture Research and Education (SARE) and organic farming groups to do on-farm research.
- Develop a program for testing and quality assurance (pH, organic matter, moisture, biological activity)
- Make marketing a significant part of the business plan and budget. This includes targeted market research
- Educational materials, package design, trade shows, and promotional events (Quillan, 1998).

11.10.7 Other Requirements

11.10.7.1 Container

The shape and size of the Vermicomposting container, depending on the requirement, is the quantity of waste to be composted and the number of live earthworms we want to culture. On average, 2000 adult earthworms can be maintained in containers of 1 m2 dimension. These with appropriate conditioning of composting material would convert approximately 200 kgs wastes every month. Interestingly, roughly in a container of 2.23 Ã— 2.23 m. about 10 kgs of earthworms can convert approximately 1 ton per month. However, to have optimal conversion normally only upper 9-12" layer is composted. This should be softly scraped off.

11.10.7.2 Containers: Types

A suitable bin can be constructed of untreated, non-aromatic wood, or plastic container to be purchased. A wooden box is better if you will keep the worms

Construction of Worm Bin

outdoors because it will keep the worms cooler in the summer and warmer in the winter. If a plastic container is used, it should be thoroughly washed and rinsed before the worms and bedding are added. The bin size depends on the amount of food produced by your household. The general rule of thumb is one square foot of surface area for each pound of garbage generated per week. For two people (producing approximately 2 kg of food scraps per week), a box 2 feet wide, 2 feet long, and 8 inches deep waste should be adequate. A 2-foot-by-3- foot box is suitable for four to six people (about 3 kg per week). Redworms (the type used for vermicomposting) thrive in moist bedding in a bin with air holes on all sides. For aeration and drainage, drill nine Â½-inch holes in the bottom of the 2-foot by- 2-foot bin or 12 holes in the 2-foot-by-3 foot bin. Place a plastic tray under the worm bin to collect any moisture that may seep out. Drilling holes on the upper sides of your bin will also help your worms get needed oxygen and prevent odors in your worm bin. Keep a lid on the bin, as worms like to work in the dark. Store the worm bin where the temperature remains between 55° and 77°F.

11.10.7.2.1 Small Barrel or Drum Composter

The barrel or drum composter generates compost in a relatively short period and provides an easy mechanism for turning. This method requires a barrel of at least 55 gallons with a secure lid. Be sure that the barrel was not used to store toxic chemicals. Drill 6-9 rows or Â½ inch holes over the length of the barrel to allow for air circulation and drainage of excess moisture. Place the barrel upright on blocks to allow bottom air circulation. Fill the barrel Â¾ full with organic waste material and add about Â¼ cup of high (approximately 30% N) nitrogen-containing fertilizer. Applying water until the compost is moist but not soggy. Every few days, turn the drum on its side and roll it around the yard to mix and aerate the compost. The lid can be removed after turning to allow for air penetration. Ideally, the compost should be ready in two to four months. The barrel composter is an excellent choice for the city dweller with a relatively small yard.

11.10.7.2.2 Large Barrel or Drum Composter

For large quantities of organic waste, bin type structures are the most practical. As an example, a circular bin can be made by using a length of small spaced woven wire fencing and holding it together with chain snaps The bin should be about three to five feet in diameter and at least four feet high. A stake may be driven in the middle of the bin before adding material to help maintain the shape of the pile and to facilitate adding water. With this design, it is easiest to turn the composting material by simply unsnapping the wire, moving the wire cylinder a few feet, and turning the compost back into it.

11.10.7.2.3 Three-chambered Bin

A very efficient and durable structure for fast composting is a three-chambered bin. It holds a considerable amount of compost and allows good air circulation. The three-chambered bin works on an assembly line idea having three batches of compost in varying stages of decomposition The compost assembly line idea, having three batches of compost in varying stages of decomposition. The compost material is started in the first bin and allowed to heat up for three to five days. Next, it is turned into the middle bin for another 4-7 days, while a new batch of material is started in the first bin. Finally, the material in the middle bin is turned into the last bin as finished or nearly finished compost.

11.10.7.2.4 Making of three-chambered bin

For this purpose use rot-resistant wood such as redwood, salt treated wood, or wood treated with an environmentally safe preservative or a combination of treated wood and metal posts. Unless the wood is treated or root resistant, it will decompose within a few years. Each bin should be at least three to five feet in each dimension to contain enough volume to compost properly. Using removable slats in the front offers complete access to the contents for turning. Initially, proper collection, sorting or separation of compostable, non-compostable, and non biodegradables like plastics, stone, glass, ceramics, and metals should be done. Heavily contaminated wastes (even in kitchen wastes, heavily spicy wastes) with chemicals should be separated. The clean matter selected for composting should be heaped and large lumps should be broken. The separated matter should be spread in a layer up to 1 foot and to be exposed to the sun for a day. This helps in killing several unwanted organisms and removes the foul smell. The mixing of daily organic waste products may be done with somewhat pretreated leaf litter in an approximate ratio ranging from 10 to 40% of the waste to be vermicomposted.

11.11 Ideal conditions for Life of Earthworms

Keep them at 55 to 70 degradation. being a good average temperature of the bedding. Mean humidity should be 55 %, and keep the earthworms out of the rain. They will drown and/or scatter all over under rainy or very humid conditions, Finally, the pH of the bed should be as close to 6.5 as possible, with 7.0 and 6.0 being the upper and lower pH limits.

11.11.1 Food for Worms

Under optimum conditions, redworms can eat their weight in food scraps and bedding in one day. On average, however, it takes approximately 2 pounds of earthworms (approximately 2,000 breeders) to recycle a pound of food waste in 24

hours. The same quantity of worms requires about 4 cubic feet of the bin to process the food waste and bedding (1 cubic foot of worm bin/500 worms). Composting worms can be purchased from dealers listed in the sections of many garden magazines. Some dealers sell worms as pit-run worms consist of worms of all ages and sizes. Add worms to the top of the moist bedding when they arrive. The worms will disappear into the bedding within a few minutes.

11.11.2 Adding Food Waste

Earthworms eat all kinds of food and yard wastes, including coffee grounds, tea bags, vegetable and fruit waste, pulverized eggshells, grass clippings, manure, and sewage sludge. Avoid bones, dairy products, and meats that may attract pests, and also avoid garlic, onions, and spicy foods. Limited amounts of citrus can be added, but too much can make the compost too acidic. The compost should be kept at a pH of 6.5 if possible, with upper and lower limits at 7.0 and 6.0, respectively. Overly acidic compost can be corrected by adding crushed eggshells. Avoid adding chemicals (including insecticides), metals, plastics, glass, soaps, pet manures, and oleanders or other poisonous plants, or plants sprayed with insecticides to the worm bin. Food wastes should be added to the bin by pulling back the bedding material and burying it. Be sure to cover it well to avoid attracting flies and other pests. Successive loads of waste should be buried at different locations in the bin to keep the food wastes from accumulating. Grinding or blending the food waste in a food processor speeds the composting time considerably.

11.11.3 Proper Ingredient Mixture

In broad terms, there are two major kinds of food that composting microbes need:

11.11.3.1 Browns

Browns are dry and dead plant materials such as straw, dry brown weeds, autumn leaves, and wood chips or sawdust. These materials are mostly made of chemicals that are just long chains of sugar molecules linked together. As such, these items are a source of energy for the compost microbes. Because they tend to be dry, browns often need to be moistened before they are put into a compost system.

11.11.3.2 Greens

Greens are fresh (and often green) plant materials such as green weeds from the garden, kitchen fruit and vegetable scraps, green leaves, coffee grounds, and tea bags, fresh horse manure, etc. Compared to browns, greens have more nitrogen in them. Nitrogen is a critical element in amino acids and proteins and can be thought

of as a protein source for the billions of multiplying microbes. A good mix of browns and greens is the best nutritional balance for the microbes. Half-and-half of greens and browns or two parts browns to one part greens works pretty well. This mix also helps out with the aeration and amount of water in the pile. Browns, for instance, tend to be bulky and promote good aeration. Greens on the other hand, are typically high in moisture, and balanced out the dry nature of the browns.

11.11.3.3. Particle Size

The smaller the size of organic wastes, the faster the compost will be ready for use. Smaller particles have much more surface area that can be attacked by microbes. A shredder can be used before putting material in the pile and is essential if brush or sticks are to be composted. A low-cost method of reducing the size of fallen tree leaves is to mow the lawn before raking or run the lawn mower over leaf piles after ranking. Raked piles should be checked to ensure that they do not contain sticks or rocks which could cause injury during the operation of the mower. If the mower has an appropriate bag attachment, the shredded leaves can be collected directly. In addition to speeding up the composting process, shredding will initially reduce the volume of the compost pile.

11.11.3.4 Fertilizer and Lime

Microbial activity is affected by the carbon to nitrogen ratio of organic waste. Because microbes require a certain amount of nitrogen for their metabolism and growth, a shortage of nitrogen will slow down the composting process considerably. Materials high in carbon relative to nitrogen such as straw or sawdust will decompose very slowly unless nitrogen fertilizer is added. Tree leaves are higher in nitrogen than straw or sawdust but the decomposition of leaves would still benefit from an addition of nitrogen fertilizer or components high in nitrogen. The grass clipping is generally high in nitrogen and when mixed properly with leaves will enhance decomposition. Poultry litter, manure, or blood meal can be used as organic sources of nitrogen. Otherwise, fertilizer with a high nitrogen analysis (10-30%) should be used. Other nutrients such as phosphorus and potassium are usually present in adequate amounts for decomposition.

11.11.3.5 pH

During the initial stages of decomposition, organic acids are produced and decrease the pH. In the past, small amounts of lime have been suggested for maintaining and enhancing microbial activity at this time. However, high rates of lime will convert ammonium nitrogen to ammonia gas, which will lead to the loss of nitrogen from the pile. Research indicated that lime additions may hasten

decomposition; however, the loss of nitrogen from the pile often offsets the benefits of lime. In general, lime is not necessary for the degradation of most yard wastes. The pH of the finished compost is usually alkaline (pH= 7.1-7.5) without the addition of lime. If large quantities of pine needles, pine bark, or vegetable and fruit wastes are composted, additional lime may be necessary.

11.12 Other factor affecting Earthworm's growth

11.12.1 Earthworm and Insects

The major earthworm predator is the mole. This voracious insect predator loves to dine on white grubs and any earthworm it can find. Grubs, attached to the root from which they gain their food, can't escape, but the earthworm can feel the vibrations of the mole digging and quickly try to flee. The moles own digging conceals the noise of the earthworm fleeing, so star nose mole developed a unique method to find earthworms. It uses its funny looking nose to detect the faint electrical fields that earthworms (and some other insects) radiate. Not only does this mole detect and find an earthworm, but it knows how to bite it so it is paralyzed but does not die. The mole stores the living worm along the burrow as food for dining at leisure. Another predator, usually not found in the northeast, is a carnivorous snail. These snails are long and thin, just right for invading the shell of another snail and devouring it. But they also love earthworms. When you till the ground, the earthworms flee the tillers vibration (They must think its BIG mole). So, the active earthworms are not usually chopped by the tiller. Some earthworms, like nightcrawlers, have 5 hearts. I chopped in half, they don't die but try to regenerate; however, sometimes a half gets confused and it ends up regenerating a worm.

11.12.2 Tilling and Earthworm Population

Tilling the soils do reduce the earthworm population. Not because it kills or disturbs them, but because tilling aerates the soil, and this oxygen quickly reduces the organic matter that the earthworm uses as food. Mulching with green matter will help provide food to earthworms to replenish what is lost in tilling. The population of earthworms, in the north, follows a different cycle than most garden fauna. The population of adults is highest in the spring, and decreases in the dry summer months, followed by an increase of young in the wetter, cooler fall. For a high number of earthworms in the spring, its important to protect the young and the eggs overwinter. Earthworms can freeze solid and still live if the freeze is slow and they do not thaw out and refreeze often, Any form of ground cover, cover crops, leaves, mulch, or even boards help mediate the freezing and allow more earthworms to survive the winter. Fields that are ploughed and left bare are almost devoid of earthworms in the spring. Luckily, earthworms have a high K (reproduction) factor.

11.12.3 Earthworm and come out to Grounding

Earthworms come out of their burrows during rain to avoid grounding. Worms have no lungs, they take their oxygen directly through the skin, either from the air or from water. Rather than fear water, they love it. It's drying out they fear and dry soil kills them. When it rains, they come to the surface because its easier to find a mate in the flat open ground than in the three-dimensional burrows. The wet ground allows them to move without fear of drying out. To an earthworm, the wet ground in a wild singles bar.

11.13 Maintaining the Bin

Food scraps can be continually added to the bin for up to 2 to 3 months, or until you notice the bedding material disappear. When the bedding disappears, harvest the worms and finished compost, then refill the bins with new bedding material.

11.13.1 Watering in Bin

Overloading the bin with food wastes can result in foul odors. If you notice these odors, stop adding the waste until the worms have a chance to catch up. Overly moist food waste and bedding also cause odors. To relieve this problem, fluff up the bedding to add air and check the drainage holes. As a general rule of thumb, keep the bedding material moist, but never soggy. Make sure the food waste is buried properly in the bedding. Exposed food wastes can attract fruit flies, house flies, and other pests. Keeping the bin covered with straw or moist burlap also deters these pests. Garden centipedes can be a problem in the worm bin, especially outside. These predators should be destroyed. Overly wet beds also can attract earthworm mite, which causes the worms to stop eating.

12
METHODS OF VERMICOMPOSTING TECHNIQUE

There are three basic types of vermicomposting systems of interest to farmers which are windrows, beds or bins, and flow-through reactors. Each type has several variants. Windrows and bins can be batch or continuous-flow systems, while all flow-through systems, as the name suggests, are of the continuous-flow variety.

12.1 Windrows

Windrow vermicomposting can be carried out in several different ways. The three most common are described here. Static pile windrows (batch) are simply piles of mixed bedding and feed or bedding with feed layered on top, that are inoculated with worms and allowed to stand until the processing is completed. These piles are usually elongated in a windrow style but can also be squares, rectangles, or any other shape that makes sense for the person building them. They should not exceed one meter in height (before settling).

Figure – 12.1: Windrows

12.2 Top-Fed Windrows

Top-fed windrows are similar to the windrows described above, except that they are not mixed and placed as a batch, but are set up as a continuous-flow operation. This means that the bedding is placed first, then inoculated with worms, and then covered repeatedly with thin (less than 10 cm) layers of food. The worms tend to consume the food at the food/bedding interface, then drop their castings near the bottom of the window. A layered windrow is created over time, with the finished product on the bottom, partially consumed bedding in the middle, and the fresher food on top. Layers of new bedding should be added periodically to replace the bedding material gradually consumed by the worms. Unlike the batch windrows described above, these windrows require continuous feeding and are difficult/ not impossible to operate in the winter.

12.3 Wedges

The vermicomposting wedge is an interesting variation on the top-fed windrow. An initial stock of worms in bedding is placed inside a corral-type structure (3-sided)15 of no more than three feet or one meter in height. The sides of the corral can be concrete, wood, or even bales of hay or straw. Fresh material is added on a regular feeding schedule through the open side, usually by a bucket loader. The worms follow the fresh food over time, leaving the processed material behind. When the material has reached the open end of the corral, the finished material is harvested by removing the back of the corral and scooping the material out with a loader. A side is then put in place and the direction is reversed. Using this system, the worms do not need to be separated from the vermicompost and the process can be continued indefinitely. During the coldest months, a layer of insulating hay or straw can be placed over the active part of the wedges. The corrals can be any width at all, the only constraint being access to the interior of the piles for monitoring and corrective actions, such as adjustment of moisture content or pH level. A corral width of about 6 feet, with space between adequate for foot travel, would be ideal. The ideal length will depend on the material being processed, the size of the worm population, and other factors affecting processing times. The sides of the corrals can be made of any material at all, although the insulating value is a consideration. Hay or straw bales will gradually break down over time and be consumed by the worms; as a bale loses its structural integrity, however, it can be added to the contents of the wedge and replaced with a fresh one.

Methods of Vermicomposting Technique

12.4 Beds or Bins

12.4.1 Top-fed beds

A top-fed bed works like a top-fed windrow. The main difference is that the bed, unlike a windrow, is contained within four walls and (usually) a floor, and is protected to some degree from the elements, often within an unheated building such as a barn. The beds can be built with insulated sides, or bales of straw can be used to insulate them in the winter. If the bins are fairly large, they are sheltered from the wind and precipitation, and the feedstock is reasonably high in nitrogen, the only insulation required may be an insulating "pillow" or layer on top. These can be as simple as bags or bales of straw. The beds built on the Scott farm have walls of mortared cinder block. They are on a concrete floor inside the chicken coop, which is the lowest level of an old barn. The area receives some heat from a greenhouse attached to the building, but winter temperatures are consistently well below freezing. The bins are covered in the winter with insulating pillows made by stuffing bats of pink fiberglass insulation inside plastic bags. During the first winter of operation, the top insulation was not added until well into the winter, when it appeared possible that the tops of the bins might freeze over. After the insulation was put on top, the bins came through a very cold winter quite well, with only a slight drop-off inefficiency. To harvest, the operator simply stops feeding one of the beds for several weeks, allowing the worms time to finish that material and then migrate to the other beds in search of fresh feed. The "cured" bed is then emptied and refilled with bedding, after which feeding is resumed. This is repeated on a regular rotating basis.

12.4.2 Stacked bins

One of the major disadvantages of the bed or bin system is the amount of surface area required. While this is also true of the windrow and wedge systems, they are outdoors, where space is not as expensive as it is undercover. Growing worms indoors or even within an unheated shelter is an expensive proposition if nothing is done to address this issue. Stacked bins address the issue of space by adding the vertical dimension to vermicomposting. The bins must be small enough to be lifted, either by hand or with a forklift, when they are full of wet material. They can be fed continuously, but this involves handling them regularly. The more economical route to take is to use a batch process, where the material is premixed and placed in the bin, worms are added, and the bin is stacked for a pre-determined length of time and then emptied. The main disadvantage of the stacked-bin system is the initial cost of set-up. It requires an unheated shelter, bins, a way to mix the bedding and feed, and equipment to stack the bins, such as a forklift. On a smaller scale, of course, this

Methods of Vermicomposting Technique

could all be done by hand. Another disadvantage arises when it comes time to harvest. As with the batch windrow systems, the worms are mixed in with the product and need to be separated. That requires either a harvester or another step in the process, where the material is piled so that the worms can migrate into new material.

12.5 Material flow for the conventional composting process

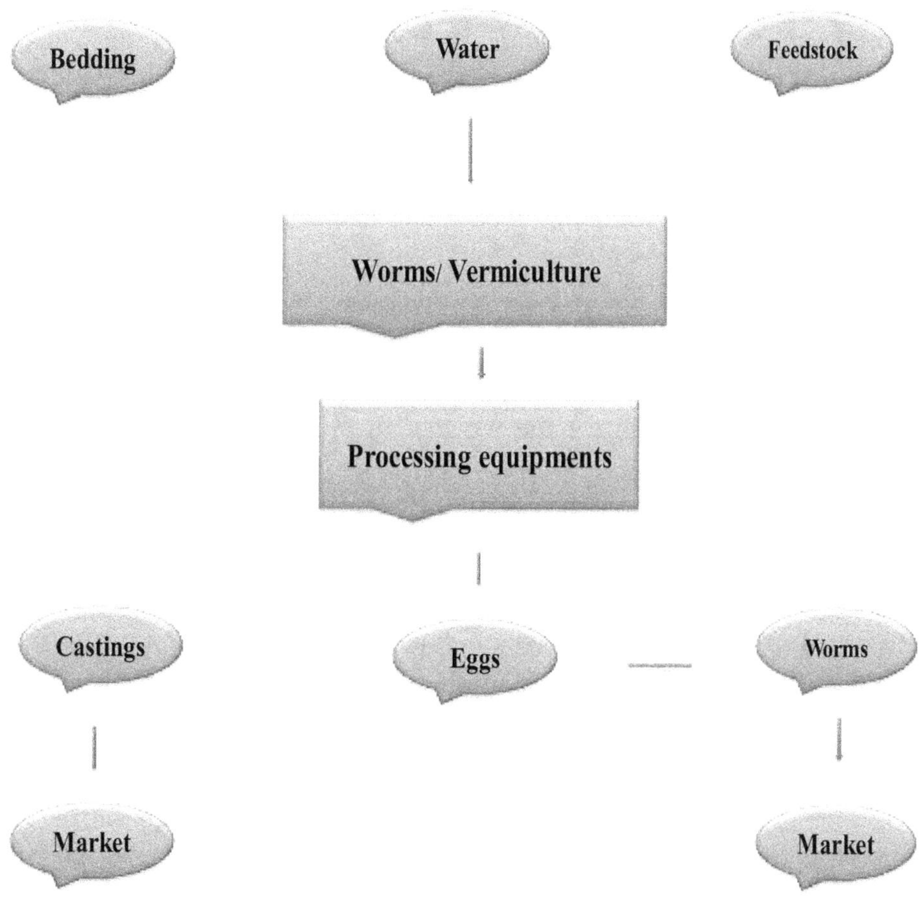

13
METHOD OF PREPARATION OF VERMICOMPOST

Vermicomposting can be done indoors and outdoors, thus allowing year-round composting. Wooden / plastic containers either build or buy or something like an old dresser drawer, trunk or disclaim: ted barrel may be used for Vermicomposting. Wooden containers preferably should be used because it is more absorbent and a better insulator for the worms. In plastic containers, compost tends to get quite wet. Containers should not be very large and heavy for easier lifting and moving. Depending on the size of the container drill 8 to 12 semicircular holes half of the inches in the bottom for aeration and drainage. A plastic bin needs more drainage holes. Raise the container on bricks or wooden blocks and place a tray underneath to capture excess liquid, which can be used as liquid plant fertilizer. The container needs a cover to conserve moisture and provide darkness for the worms. If the container is indoors, a sheet of dark plastic placed loosely on top of the bedding is sufficient as a cover. For outdoor containers, a solid lid should be preferred, to keep away unwanted scavengers and rain. Worms need air to live, so be sure to have bin sufficiently ventilated. It is necessary to provide damp bedding for the worms to live in, and to burry food waste in. Suitable bedding materials are cow dung slurry, shredded newspaper and cardboard, shredded fall leaves, chopped up straw, and other dead plants, seaweed, sawdust, compost, and aged manure. It is very important to moisten the dry bedding materials before putting them in the container. Do not use large size worms found in soil and compost, as they are not likely to survive. It is advisable not to compost meats, dairy products, oily foods, and grains because of problems with smells, flies, and rodents. No glass, plastic, or tin foil should be present in the composting materials. Containers should be kept out of the hot sun and heavy rain. If the temperature drops below 40 degrees F, containers should be replaced indoors or well-insulated outdoors. It is estimated that 1000 tonnes of

sludge organic waste could be converted into 400 tonnes of organic fertilizer through vermicomposting. A flow chart for the preparation of Vermicompost is given here with containers preferably should be used because it is more absorbent and a better insulator for the worms. In plastic containers, compost tends to get quite wet. Containers should not be very large and heavy for easier lifting and moving. Depending on the size of the container drill 8 to 12 semicircular holes half the inches in the bottom for aeration and drainage. A plastic bin needs more drainage holes. Raise the container on bricks or wooden blocks and place a tray underneath to capture excess liquid, which can be used as liquid plant fertilizer.

13.1 Materials required for Vermicomposting for a 10 sq.m. Plot

Stone chips of 1 cm size	For the filling of pit 3"
Stand or Morang	For the filling of pit 3"
Wet soil	For the filling of pit 6"
Dry organic matter	200-300kg
Decomposed Farmyard Manure	300-400kg
Organic waste including kitchen waste	700-800kg
Earthworms	10,000
Water	Ready supply

13.2 Comparative Statement of Farmyard Manure and Vermicompost

Particularls	Farmyard manure	Vermicomposting
Nitrogen %	0.40-0.75	1.00-1.60
Phosphorous %	0.17-0.30	0.50-5.04
Potash %	0.20-0.55	0.80-1.50
Calcium %	0.91	0.44
Magnesium %	0.19	0.15
Iron (ppm)	146.50	175.20
Manganese (ppm)	69.00	96.51
Zink (ppm)	14.50	24.43
Copper (ppm)	2.80	4.89
Carbon: Nitrogen Ratio	31.28	15.50
Duration required for the preparation	One year	Less than ¼th year
Immunity against insect pest and diseases	Not Developed	Developed

13.3. Preparation of Vermicompost

- **STEP – 1:** Prepare the pit 1.5 m × 1.0 m × 0.75 m without flooring and make Proper arrangement of shade
- **STEP – 2:** Fill up the pit 3" by concrete (small stones)
- **STEP – 3:** Fill up the pit 3" by sand/morang
- **STEP – 4:** Fill up the pit 6" by moist soil
- **STEP – 5:** Release earthworm @ 20 number or 20 gm/kg; or 1 kg/1000 sq mt or /50 kg or 20000 earthworm / MT organic waste
- **STEP – 6:** Placement of cow dung heap
- **STEP – 7:** Fill up the pit 4" by agro waste
- **STEP – 8:** Cover with gunny bag or coconut leaf
- **STEP – 9:** Provide water up to 30 days daily and wait
- **STEP – 10:** Remove cover of gunny bag or coconut leaf
- **STEP – 11:** Fill up pit 3" with cow dung and agro waste twice in a week followed by covering and watering
- **STEP – 12:** Turning of compost once in a week
- **STEP – 13:** Continue the process of filling covering, watering and turning up to the completion of pit
- **STEP – 14:** After complete filling of pit continue watering up to 45 days and turning once in a week
- **STEP – 15:** Stop watering for 2 days
- **STEP – 16:** Remove the compost from the pit
- **STEP – 17:** Make a heap in Shady place for 3 days
- **STEP – 18:** Collect the worm from the lower level of heap and again release them in the pit
- **STEP – 19:** Sieving and packing of Vermicompost

14

VERMIWASH

Vermiwash is the liquid extraction that is collected after the passage of water through a column of earthworm worked out compost. This extract has solubilized NPK, micronutrients, organic molecules, some hormones/ enzymes, which stimulate the growth and yield of crops and even develop resistance in crops receiving the spray. It is a commercial product. This liquid is collected in the form of liquid from the culture tanks and used as a foliar application. One of the methods that are followed is to have an outlet and an inner vessel. The inner vessel will have an outlet at the low side of the vessel. The inner vessel is filled with decomposing organic matter and about 1 to 2 kg earthworms are accommodated in 12 to 16 L capacity vessels. When the earthworms started feeding on the waste, water is slowly added into the vessel in excess. The excess water flows through the outlet in the form of thick syrupy fluid which is collected in the outer vessel. The fluid so collected is siphoned out and after diluting, is used as a foliar spray to different crops. In some farmlands, the tank is built at an elevated place from which wash is to be collected. The slope provided in the tank provides scope for excess water to flow out in drops as thick syrupy emulsion through a small outlet. The fluid is collected and stored in bottles. It is diluted before using and then sprayed to crops.

14.1 Vermiwash - A plant growth regulator

Vermiwash is a liquid plant growth regulator that contains a high amount of enzymes, vitamins, and hormones like auxins, gibberellins, etc. along with macro and micro-nutrients.

14.2 Method of Preparation

Take one big bucket and one mug. Set up one stopcock on the lowermost part of the bucket. Put a layer of broken brick pieces of stones having a thickness of 10-15 cm in the bucket. Over this layer put another layer of sand having a thickness of 10-15 cm. Then put a layer partially decomposed cow dung having 30-45 cm thickness over it. Then put another layer of soil having 2-3 cm thickness. Now open the stop cock of the bucket and water the materials taken in the bucket. Method of

preparation: Then put 100-200 nos. of earthworms in the bucket. After that, a layer of paddy straw having 6 cm thickness is given. Now open the stopcock of the bucket and spray water regularly for 7-8 days. After 10 days the liquid Vermiwash will be produced in the bucket. Hang one pot with a bottom hole over the bucket in such a way so that water falls drop by drop. Every day 4-5 liters of water are to be poured in the hanging pot. Keep another pot below the stopcock to collect the Vermiwash. Every day 3-4 liters of liquid Vermiwash can be collected.

14.3 Application

Mix 1 liter of vermiwash with 7-10 liters of water and spray the solution in the leaf (upper and lower side) in the evening at the growing stage of the crop. Mix 1 liter of vermiwash with 1 liter of cow urine and then add 10 liters of water to the vermicompost solution and mix thoroughly and keep it overnight before spraying. 50 to 60 liters of such a solution are to be sprayed in $1/5^{th}$ acre of land to control various crop diseases.

15

CONCLUSION

In recent years, the ecological characteristics and beneficial effects of earthworm have been demonstrated, focused by scientific research. Worms can be used to process animal waste that was considered a potential environmental problem. Earthworm's activity influences the rate of soil turnover, mineralization, and humification of soil organic matter. Improvement in the consistency of soil texture with a concomitant increase in porosity, infiltration, and soil water retention are other characteristics of worm-worked soils. There are multiple benefits of Vermitechnology, low-cost production of biofertilizer, environmental management of solid wastes, and agricultural residues enhanced soil productivity, tastier quality food, among others. Vermitechnology also aids in the reduction of soil salinity, soil erosion with less runoff, and wasteland development. From this present review, it is concluded that the organic wastes are effectively recycled by microorganisms followed by earthworms and plays a major role in the development of growth and yield of crops. The nutritive value of compost material is high and the composting process effectively converts the waste product into useful by-products. Raise worms on a small scale first. Create business and marketing plans based on your experience and thorough research. Always remember that you will have to sell your product to create a commercial enterprise. Concentrate on combining the satisfaction of raising worms in a sustainable system with a profitable business model. Vermicomposting can produce high-quality fertilizers which are better compared to other commercial fertilizers in the market.

16
RECOMMENDATIONS

- Nowadays precise doses of allergenic, pathogens, and toxins have not been defined, which have harmful effects on human health and environment. To determine the influence of excessive concentrations of allergens and pathogens in workers' health involved in composting, it is necessary to carry on additional long-term epidemiological studies of the composting.
- More and more citizens are engaged in waste composting on a small scale. Taking into consideration that these systems are conducted by an extensive method, hygienic handling of composts with high temperatures cannot always be guaranteed. A hygienic control of such systems is required.
- Composting is a complicated complex biological process. Further research is needed to control effectively the parameters (aeration, tedding, and others), which play an important role in the optimal degradation of waste, cleaning, and maturation of compost.
- A union of research institutes, enterprises, and agencies involved in composting should lead to the establishment of "a good practice of composting". The information about possible occupational hazards for workers employed in composting should be available not only for health professionals but also for those who work with organic waste.
- When working with compost good personal hygiene should be observed: work in overalls, gloves (cotton, rubber). All works on the processing and packaging of composts should be performed in special clothes, using a respirator. Washing of overhauls should be carried out when it gets dirty.
- People engaged in the production of compost should observe good personal hygiene and mandatory undergo periodic medical examinations.
- All production facilities and workplaces should possess a first aid kit.

- All specially developed requirements and precautions should be followed while storing or transporting the composts. To develop specific recommendations for waste management and compost, to control their hygiene and agronomic properties, it is necessary to provide further joint researches of microbiologists, allergists, epidemiologists, and specialists in the field of composting.

17

REFERENCES

Abassi SA, Nayeem-Shah M, Abassi, T (2015). Vermicomposting of phytomass: limitations of the past approaches. Journal of the Cleaner Production. 93:103-105.

Appelbof, M. 1980. Vermicomposting on a household scale. *In : Soil biol.ogy as related to land use practices: Proc. Vlllntn. Colloq. Soil. Zool.,* 157-160. (Ed.) E.L. Dindal EPA, Washington.

Atlavinyte, O. & Vanagas, J. 1982. The effect of earthworms on the quality of barley and rye grain. *Pedobiologia,* 23 : 256-262.

Atlavinyte, O., Daciulyte, J. & Luganska, A. 1971. Correlation between the number of earthworms, microorganisms and vitamin B12 in soil fertilized with straw. *Liet. TSR Molesl". A/cad. Darb., sere B,* 3 : 43-56.

Bahl, K. N. 1950. *The Indian Zoological Memoirs. 1. Pheretima.* 4th edition. Lucknow Publishing House, Lucknow.

Bahl, KN. (1927). On other productive process of earthworms: Part I. The process of copulation and exchange of sperms in *E-utyphoeus waltoni. Q.J.micros. Sci.,* 71 : 479-502.

Bhaduria,T. & Ramakrishnan, P. S. 1989. Earthworm population dynamics and contribution to nuttient cycling during cropping and fallow phases of shifting agriculture (Jhum) in Northeast India. *J. Appl. Ecol.,* 26 : 505-520.

Bouch, M. B. 1977. Strategies lombriciennes. *Ecol. Bull. (Stockholm), 2S* : 122-132.

Bouche, M. 1977. Strategies lombriciennes. *Ecol. Bull. (Stockholm),* 25 : 122-132.

Burges, A. and Raw, F. 1967. *Soil Biology.* Academic Press, London & New York.

Byzova, J.A. 1965. Comparative role of respiration in some earthworms (Lumbricidae, Oligochaeta). *Rev. Ecol. Bioi. Sol.,* 2 : 207-216.

Darwin. C. 1881. *The formation of vegetable mould through the action of worms, with observations on their habits.* Murray, London.

Dash, M. C. & Senapati, B. K. 1982. Environmental regulation of oligochaete reproduction in topical pastures. *Pedobiologia,* 23 : 270-271.

Dash, M.C. & Patra U.C. 1977. Density biomass and energy budget of a tropical earthworm population from a grassland site in Orissa, India. *Rev. Ecol. Bioi. Sol.,* 14 : 461-471.

Dash, M.C. & Senapati, B.K. 1986. Vermitechnology, an option for organic waste management in India *In : Proc. Nat. Sem. Org. Waste Utilize Vermicomp .. Part B. Verms and Vermicomposting,* 157-172 (Eds.) M.C. Dash, B.K. Senapati & P.C. Mishra. Sri Artattana Rout for Five Star Printing Press, Burla, Orissa.

Deoksen, J. 1950. An electrical method of sampling soil for earthworms. *Trans. 4th Int. Congr. Soil Sci.* : 129-131.

Dickinson, C. H. &. Pugh, G. J. F. 1974. *Biology of plant litter decomposition.* Vols. 1, 2. Academic Press, London & New York.

Dutt, A. K. 1948. Earthworms and soil aggregation. *J. Am. Soc. Agron.,* 48 : 407.

Edwards CA and Lofty JR, Nitrogenous fertilizers and earthworm population in the agricultural soil, *Soil Biology and Biochemistry*, 1982, 14, 515-521.

Edwards, C. A. & Thompson, A. R. 1973. Pesticides and soil fauna. *Residue Rev.,* 4S : 1-79.

Edwards, C. A. &. Lofty, J. R. (1972). *Biology of earthworms,* Chapman and Hall, London, 283 pp.

Edwards, C. A., Reichle, D. E. &. Crossley, D. A. J. 1970. The role of soil invertebrates in turn over of organic matter and nutrients .. ln : *Ecological studies, Analysis and Synthesis,* 1, 147-172. (Ed.) D. E. Reichle.

Edwards. C. A. & Lofty, J. R. 1977. *Biology of earthworms,* 2nd edition. Chapman and Hall, London.

Evans, A. C. & Guild, W. J. Mc.L. (1948a). Studies on the relationship between worms and soil fertility. IV .. On the life cycles of some British Lumbricidae. *Ann. apple Bioi.,* 35 : 471-484.

Evans, A. C. & Guild, W. J. Mc.L. (1948b). Studies on the relationships between earthworms and soil fertility. V. Field populations. *Ann. apple Bioi.,* 3S : 485-493.

Evans, A. C. & Guild, W. j. McL. 1948. Studies on the relationship between earthworms and soil fertility. IV. On the life cycles of some British Lumbricidae. *Ann. Appl. Bioi.,* 35 : 471--484.

Fewell, Roy and Dianne Fewell. 2007. As the Worm Turns: New and Easy Methods for Raising Earthworms. Shields Publications, PO Box 669, Eagle River, WI 54521. p. 43.

Gaddie, Ronald E., Sr. and Donald E. Douglas. 1975. Earthworms for Ecology & Profi t. Volume I: Scientifi c Earthworm Farming. Bookworm Publishing Co., PO Box 3037, Ontario, CA 91761. p. 59.

Gadgil, M. &. Bossett, W. (1970). Life history consequences of natural selection. *Amer. Nat.,* 104 : 1-24.

Galli, E., Tomati, V., Grappelli, A. & Di Lena, G. 1990. Effect of earthworm cast in protein synthesis in *Agaricus bisporus. Bioi F.ertil. Soil,* 9 : 1-2.

Gandhi M, Sangwan V, Kapoor KK and Dilbaghi N, Composting of household wastes with and without earthworms, *Environment and Ecology,* 1997, 15(2), 432–434.

Garg P, Gupta A, and Satya S, Vermicomposting of different types of waste using *Eisenia foetida*: A comparative study, *Bioresource Technology,* 2006, 97, 391-395.

Gates, G. E. 1929. A summary of earthworm fauna of Burma with descriptions of 14 new species. *Proc. U. S.' natn. Mus.,* 75 (1) : 1-41.

Gates, G. E. 1930. The earthwonns of Burma. I. *Rec. Indian Mus.,* 32 : 257-356.

Gates, G. E. 1931. The earthworms of Burma II. *Rec. Indian Mus.,* 33 : 327-442.

Gates, G. E. 1932. The earthworms of Burma. III. *Rec. Indian Mus.,* 34 : 357-549.

Gates, G. E. 1933. The earthworms of Burma IV. *Rec. Indian Mus.,* 3S : 413-606.

Gates, G. E. 1945. On some Indian earthworms. ll. 11. *R. Asiat. Soc. Beng.,* 11 (1) : 54-91.

Gates, G. E. 1972. Burmese earthworms. An introduction to the systematics and biology of' megadrile oligochaetes with reference to South Asia. *Trans. Am. phil. Soc.,* 62 (7) : l- 326.

Grove, A. J., & L. F .Cowley (1926). Quart. J. Microscop. Sci. 70 : 559 *In* : *Chemical Zoology,* ChI Growth and Development, (Eds.) M. Plorkin and B. T. Scheer. Vol. IV. Academic Press London.

Gurrero, R. D. 1983. The culture and use of *Perionyx excavatus* as a prqtein resouce in the Philipines.ln : *Earthworm Ecology from Darwin to Vermiculture* : 309-313. (Ed.) J. E. Satchell. Chapman and Hall, London.

Hartenstein, RN., Edwards, N.F. & Kaplan, D.L. 1979. A progress r~port on the potential use of earthworms in sludge management. *In* : *Proc. VIII-Natn. Sludge Con!* Information

Hoonweg D, Bhada-Tata P (2012) What a Waste: A Global Review of Solid Waste Management. Urban Development Series. The World Bank, Washington DC, USA

Ireland, M. P. 1977. Heavy worms. *New Sci.,* 76 (1076) : 486-487.

Joshi, N. V. & Kelkar, B. V. 1952. Role of earthworms in soil fertility. *Indian J. Agric. Sci.,* 72: 189-196.

JuJka. J. M. 1988. *The Fauna of India and adjacent countries.* Megadrile Oligochaeta (Earthworms): Haplotaxida : Lumbricina : Megascolecoidea : Octochaetidae. Zoological Survey of India, Calcutta.

Julka, J. M. 1976a. Studies on the earthworm fauna of Orissa (India) 1. Moniligastridae and 9cnerodrilidae. *Mitt. zool. Mus. Berlin,* 52 (2) : 321-329.

Julka, J. M. 1976b. Studies on the earthworms collected dwing the Daphabum expedition in Arunachal Pradesh, India. *Rec. zool. Surv. India,* 69:' 229-239.

Julka, J. M. 1978. Studies on the earthworm fauna of Orissa (India). 2. Megascolecidae, Octochaetidae and Microchaetidae. *Mitt. zool. Mus. Berlin,* 54 : 185-197.

Julta, J. M. 1981. Taxonomic studies on the earth worms collected, during the S ubansiri Expedition in Arunachal Pradesh, India. *Rec. zool. Surv. India. Dcc. Paper,* No. 26 : 1-

Kale, R. D. & Bano, K. (1985) Laboratory propagation of some indigenous species of earthworms. *J. Soil Bioi. Ecol.,* 5 (1) : 20-25.

Kale, R. D. & Bano, K. 1988. Earthworm cultivation and culturing technique for production of Vee compo 83 E UAS' 'and 'Vee meal 83P UAS' *Mys. J. agri Sci.,* 22

Kale, R. D. & Krishnamoorthy, R. V. 1981. Litter preference in earthworm *Lampito mawitii. Proc. Indian Acad. Sci.,* 90 : 125-128.

Kale, R. D. 1986. Earthwonn feed for poUltry and aquaCUlture. *In : Proc. Nat. Sem. Org. Waste Utilize Vermicomp. Part B, Verms and Vermicomposling,* 137-144. (Eds.) M. C. Dash, B. K. Senapati and P. C. Mishra. Sri Artatrana Rout for Five Star Printing Press, Burla, Orissa.

Kale, R. D., Bano, K. & Krishnamoorthy, R. V. (1982) Potential of *Perionyx* excavatus for utilizing organic wastes. *Pedobiologia,* 23 : 419-425.

Kale, R. D., Bano, K., Sreenivasa, M. N., Vinayak, K. & Bagyaraj, D. J .. (in press). Incidence of cellulelytic and Lignolytic organisms in the earthworm 'worked soils. *In : Proc. X Int. Zool. Co.llq., Bangalore,* 1988 : (Eds.) O. K. Veeresh, D. Rajagopal and Virekhthamath.

Kale, R. D., Mahesh, B. G., Bano, K. & Bagyaraj, D. I. (in press). Influence of Vermicompost application on the available macronutrients and selected microbial populations in a paddy field. *In : Proc. IV Int. Symp. On Earthworms, Avignon, France, June 1990.*

Kale, R. D.,.Bano, K., Sreenivasa, M. N. & Bagyaraj, D. J. 1987. Influence of worm cast (Vee compo E, UAS, 83) qn the growth and micorrhizal colonization of two ornamental plants. *South Ind. Hort.,* 3S : 433-437.

Kale, R.D. & Bano, K. 1986. Field trials with vermicompost (Vee compo E. 83 USA) an organic fertiliser. *In : Proc. Nat. Sem. Org. Waste Utilize Vermicomp., Part B. Verms & Vermicomposting,* 151-156. (Eds.) M.C. Dash, B.K. Senapati & P.C. Mishra. Sri Artattana Rout for Five Star Printing Press, Burla, Orissa.

Karsten ER, Making a high-quality compost tea, *Biocycle,* 1995, 40: 94.

Karthikeyan V, Sathymoorthy GL, and Murugesan R, Vermicomposting of market waste in Salem, Tamil Nadu, India. Proceedings of the international conference on sustainable solid waste management, Chennai, India, 2007, pp. 276-281.

Khaliq A, Abbasi MK and Hussain A, Effects of integrated use of organic and inorganic nutrient sources with Effective Microorganisms (EM) on seed cotton yield in Pakistan, *Bioresource Technology,* 2006, 97, 967-972.

Kuhnelt. W. 1976. *Soil Biology.* Faber and Faber, London.

Lalander CH, Komakech AJ, Vinnerås B (2015) Vermicomposting as manure management strategy for urban small-holder animal farms – Kampala case study. Waste Manage. 39:96–103.

Lavelle. P. 1983. *Agastrodrilus* Omodeo & Vaillaud, a genus of carnivorous earthworms from the Ivory Coast *In : Earthworm Ecology from 'Darwin to Vermiculture,* 425-429. (Ed.) J. E. Satchell. Chapman and Hall, New York and London.

Lee, K. E. (1985). *Earthworms. Their ecology and relationships with soils and Land use.* Academic Press, New York. 411 pp.

Lee, K. E. 1985. *Earthworms. Their ecology and relationships with soils and land use.* Academic Press, Sydney.

Lim SL, Lee LH, Wu TY (2016) Sustainability of using composting and vermicomposting technologies for organic waste biotransformation: recent overview, greenhouse gases emissions and economic analysis. Journal of Cleaner Production. 11; 262-278.

Lim SL, Wu TY, Lim PN, Shak KPY (2014) The use of vermicompost in organic farming: overview, effects on soil and economics. Journal of Science Food and Agriculture. 95; 1143- 1156.

Lim, PN, Wu, TY, Clarke, C, Daud NNN (2015) A potential bioconversion of empty fruit bunches into organic fertilizer using Eudrilus eugeniae International Journal of Environmental Science and Technology. 12 (8); 2533-2544.

Mathur RS, Magu SP, Sadisavam KV and Gaur AC, Accelerated compost and improved yields, *Biocycle*, 1986, 42-44.

Mba, C. 1978. Influence of different mulch treatments on the growth rate and activity of the earthworm *E.udrilus eugeniae* (Kinberg). Z. *pjlanzenernachr. Bodenkd.,* 141 : 453-468.

Mba, C. C. 1983. Utilisation of *Eudrilus eugeniae* for disposal of cassava peel. *In .' Earthworm ecology, from Darwin to Vermiculture".* (Ed.) I. E. Satchell. Chapman and Hall, London.

Michaelsen, W. 1909. The Oligochaeta of India, Nepal, Ceylon, Burma, and Andaman Islands. *Mem. Indian Mus.,* 1 : 103-253.

Michon, J. (1954). Influence de i - isolement a partir de la maturite sexuelle sur in biologie des Lumbricidae. C. *r. hebd. Seance Acad. Sci., Paris,* 238 : 2457-2458.

Mitchell, M. J. & Homer, S. C. 1980. Decomposition process in sewage sludge an" sludge amended soils. *In: Soil Biology as related to land use practices. Proc. 7th Intn. Colloq. Soil. Zool., New York:* 129-138. (Ed.) D. L. Dindal. Office of Pesticides and Toxic Substances, EPA, Washington, D.C.

Nair J, Sekiozoic V, and Anda M, Effect of pre-composting on vermicomposting of kitchen waste, *Bioresource Technology*, 2006, 97, 2091-2095.

Nandeesha, M. C., Srikant, G. K., Basavaraja, N., Keshavanath, P., Verghese, T. *I.,* Bano, K., Roy, A. K. & Kale, R. D. 1988. Influence of earthworm meal on growth and flesh quality of common carp. *Biological Wastes,* 26 : 188-198.

Nauhauser, F., Hartenstein, R., & Kaplan, D. L. 1980. Growth of earthworm *Eisenia /etida* in relation to population density and food rationing. *Oikos,* 3S : 93-98.

Needham, A. E. (1969). Growth and development. *In .' Chemical Zoology* (Eds.) M. Floricin and B. T. Scheer, Vol. IV. Academic Press London. p. 371-441.

Oishi, M.(1930). On the reproductive process of the earthworm *Pheretima communissima. Sci. Rep. Tohoku. Imp. Univ.,* S.

Olive, P. J. W. & Clark, R. B. (1978). Physiology of reproduction *In .' Physiology of Annelids.* (Ed.) P. J. Mill. Academic Press. London. pp. 271-368.

Phillipson, J. & Bolton, P. J. (1,977). Growth and cocoon production by *Allolobophora rosea* (OligocJtru:ta : Lurribrioidae). *Pedobioiogia,* 17: 70-82.

Pianka, E.R. 1978. *Evolutionary Ecology.* 2nd edition. Harper and Row,·New York.

Prabhat Pramanik and Young Ryun Chung, Changes in the fungal population of fly ash and vinnase mixture during vermicomposting: Documentation of cellulase isozyme in vermicompost, *Waste Management*, 2011, 1-7.

Quillian, Mike. 1998. Earthworm castings the key to unleashing the vermiculture market. Worm Digest. August. p. 13, 25, 27, 29-30. Slocum, Kelly. 2000. Going Sour on Lime. Worm Digest. No.24. p. 20.

Reinecke, A. J. & Hallat, ·L. 1989. Growth and cocoon production of *Perionyx excavates* (Oligochaeta). *Bioi. Fertil. Soil,* 8: 303-306.

Reynolds, J. W. 1977. *The. earthworms (Lumbricidae and Sparganophilidae) of Ontario.* Royal Ontario Museum, Toronto.

Rosa, D. 1894. Perichetini nouvi meno noti. *Atti. Acad. Sci. Torino,* 29 : 1-18.

Roy, S. K. 1957. Studies on the activities of earthworms. *Proc. zool. Soc., Calcutta,* 10(2) : 81- 88.

Sahu, S. K. & Senapati B. K. (1988). Alternative proposals for quantification of reproduction in tropical earthwonn. *Trop. Ecol.* 29 : 6-14.

Sahu, S. K. & Senapati, B. K. (1986). Population density, dynamic~, reproductive biology and secondary production of *Dichogaster bolaui* (Michaelsen). *Proc. Nat. Sem. Org. Waste Utilize and Vermicomp.,* M. C. Dash, B. K. Senapati and P. C. Mishra (Eds.) Five Star Printing Press, Burla. pp. 97-110.

Sahu, S. K. & Senapati, B. K. (1991). Reproductive strategy of a 'r' selected and 'K' selected earthworm from tropical pastures of Orissa. India. *In : Advances in Management find Conservation of Soil Fauna.* (Eds.) O. K.' Veeresh, D. Rajagopal, C. A. Viraktamath, Oxford and IBH Publ. Co. PvL' Ltd. New Delhi, 665-669.

Satchell, J. E. (1967). Lumbricidae, *In : Soil Biology,* A. Burgess and F. Raw (Eds.)., Academic Press, London., pp. 259-322.

Seastedt. T. R. 1984. The role of mioroarthropods in decomposition and mineralization processes. *Ann. Rev. Ent.,.* 29 : 25-46.

Senapati, B. k & Dash, M. C. (1984). Influence of soil temperature and moisture on the reproductive activity of tropical pasture earthworms of Orissa *J. Soil Bioi. Ecol.,* 4 : 13-21.

Senapati, B. K., Dash, H. K. & Dash, M. C. (1919). Seasonal dynamics and emergence pattern of a tropical earthworm *drawida calebi(Oligochaeta). Int. J. Invertebr. Reprod.,* 1 : 211- 277.

Senapati, B. K., Dash, M. C., Rana, A. K .. & Panda B. K. (1980)., Observation on the effect of earthworm in the decomposition process in soil under laboratory conditions. *Compo Physiol. Ecol.,* S : 140-142.

Senapati, B.K. & Dash, M.C. 1982. Earthworm as waste conditioner. lntn. *Engin. J.,* 11 : 53-57.

Senapati, B.K. & Dash. 1984. Functional role of earthwonns in decomposer subsystem. *Trop. Ecol.,* 25 (2) : 54-73.

Senapati, B.K., Pani, S.C. & Kabi, A. 1985. Effects of earthworms and green manuring on paddy production in pot culture. *In Proc. Nat. Sem. current Trends in Soil biology, 71-75,* (Eds.) M'.M. Mishra & K.K. Kapoor, Haryana Agriculture University, Hissar.

Senapti, B. K. & Dash, M. C. (1982). Earthworm as a waste conditioners. *Ind. Eng. J.,* XJ(2) 53-57.

Singh RP, Embrandiri A, Ibrahim MH, Esa N (2011b) Management of Biomass residues generated from oil palm mill; vermicomposting a sustainable option. Resour. Conserv. Recy 55:423-434.

Singh RP, Singh P, Araujo ASF, Ibrahim MH, Sulaiman O (2011a) Management of Urban solid waste: vermicomposting a sustainable option. Resour. Conserv. Recy. 55:719– 729.

Springett, J. A. & Syers, J. K. 1979. The effect of earthworm casts on rye grass seedlings. *In : Proc.ll Australasian Con/. Grassl. Invert. Ecol.* : 44-47. (Eds~) T. 1(. Crosby and R. P. Pettinger. Govt. Printer, Wellington.

Stephenson, J. (1930). *The Oligochaeta* : Oxford University press, 978 pp.

Stephenson, J. 1914 .. On a collection of Oligochaeta, mainly from Northern India. *Rec. Indian Mus.,* 10 : 321-365.

Stephenson, J. 1920. On a collection of Oligochaeta from the lesser known parts of India and eastern Persia. *Mem. Indian Mus.* 7 : 191-261.

Stephenson, J. 1921. Oligochaeta from Manipur, the Laccadive Islands, Mysore and other parts of India. *Rec. Indian. Mus.,* 22 :(745-768).

Stephenson, J.1923. *The Fauna 0/ British India including Ceylon and Burma. Oligochaeta.* Taylor and Francis, London.

Tembe, V. B. & Dubash, P. J. (1961). The Earthworms: a review. *J. Bombay nat. Hist. Soc.,* S8 : 171-201.

Tomati, 0., Galli, E., Grappelli, A. & Dilena, G. 1990. Effects of earthworm cast on protein synthesis in radish *(Raphanus sativum)* and lettuce *(Lactuga sativa)* seedlings. *Bioi. Fertil. Soils,* 9 : 1-2.

Transfer Inc., Silver Spring, Maryland.

Vail. V. A. 1972. Natural history and reproduction of *Diplocardia mississippiensis* (Oligochaeta). *Bull. Tall Timbers Res. Stn.,* no. 11 : 1-34.

Venkatachalaiah BK, The role of Karnataka compost development corporation Ltd., In Organic farming. Abstract, National seminar on organic farming and sustainable agriculture, October 9-11, APOF, Banglore, 1996, 24-25.

Vikram Reddy A, Gopappleth Gath and Rossi M, Fertilizers from vermiculture as an option for organic wastes recovery, *Agrochemical,* 2009, 27 (3), 244-251.

Viljoen, S. A. & Reinecke, A. J. 1989. The number, size and growth of hatchings of the African Nightcrawler, *Eudrilus eugeniae* (Oligochaeta). *Rev. Ecol. Bioi. Sol.,* 26 : 1-12.

Wallwork, J. A. 1970. *Ecology of soil animals.* Mcgraw-hill, London.

Walton, W. R. 1933. The reaction of earthworms to alternating currents of electricity in the soil. *Proc. enl. Soc. Wash.,* 3S : 24-27.

Watanabe, H., Hatteri,-!., Yamazaki, K., Takai, R. & Hasegawa, H. 1982. Effect of excrement of earthworm. on deodorization of ammonia. *J. Tokyo Univ. Fish.,* 69 : 11-18.

Wu, TY, Lim, SL, Lim, PN, Shak, KPY (2014) Biotransformation of biodegradable solid wastes into organic fertilizers using composting or/and vermicomposting. Chemical Engineering Transactions. 39;1579-1584.

Yasir M, Aslam Z, Kim Lee SW, Joen CO and Chung YR, Bacteria community composition, and chitinase gene diversity of vermicompost with antifungal activity. *Bioresource Technology,* 2009, 100, 4396–4403.

Zhang W., Hendrix P. F., Dame L. E., Burke R. A., Wu J., Neher D.A., Li J., Shao Y., Fu S (2013) Earthworms facilitate carbon sequestration through unequal amplification of carbon stabilization compared with mineralization. Nature Communications. 4:2576.